Instructional Design for Mortals

Don Jones

Instructional Design for Mortals

Don Jones

ISBN 9781983165863

Also By Don Jones

The DSC Book

The PowerShell Scripting and Toolmaking Book

Become Hardcore Extreme Black Belt PowerShell Ninja Rockstar

Be the Master

Don Jones' PowerShell 4N00bs

Don Jones' The Cloud 4N00bs

To everyone who's ever helped me learn. Which is basically everyone. Thank you.

Contents

Part 5: Nine Learning Killers

Part 6: How I Design: a Case Study

CONTENTS

Introduction

I taught my first formal class in 1996, and wrote my first classroom courseware in 1998. I immediately fell in love with teaching, writing, and instructional design. As many people do when they fall in love with something, I started trying to learn everything I could about it. This was before Amazon and E-Z online access to Every Book Ever Written, of course, but I tried not to let that stop me.

Sadly, I encountered a lot of hurdles. Most of what I was able to dig up at the library and bookshops was extremely academic, and frankly hard (and boring) to read. It required a lot of instructional design background that I, having never even attended college, didn't have and didn't have the patience to acquire. The few books I did find that were written for a non-academic audience were *so* incredibly condescending in tone, I couldn't make it through more than a few pages at a time. "So you want to learn about instructional design? Well, good for you! It is a very challenging yet rewarding topic, and you are making a good first step on what will be a wonderful journey!" Blurgh.

I tried not to let it deter me. I devoured what I could find on cognitive science, instructional design, and more. I learned to gleefully differentiate between *pedagogy* and *andragogy*, and eventually learned that nobody cared about the difference, which initially struck me as a problem, and then I got over it. I practiced on my students, and over time refined a set of instructional design guidelines for myself. I shared those in *The Nine Principals of Immediately Effective Instruction*, a book still available for free on my website, DonJones.com. Professionally, I moved into a position that focused heavily on instructional design, and had access to even more guinea pigs and data gathering, and wrote more than a few internal documents on better design and delivery.

This book is the result. It's as plain-English as I can make it, and as outcome-oriented as I can manage. It's got plenty of theory, but I back it up with actionable things you can do in your everyday life as someone who shares skills and knowledge. I'm a big fan of checklists, and while this book doesn't really *have* any checklists per se, it's definitely laid out in a checklist-style fashion. If you've read any of my earlier, less-formally published works, you'll recognize plenty of familiar things, but you'll also see a lot more. Hopefully, you'll find everything to be better organized for a more "what can I actually do" mindset.

I hope you find it helpful.

Let's Define Instructional Design

The phrase *instructional design* has been co-opted by a lot of different stakeholders over the years, so let me just explain how *I* use the term in this book.

For me, instructional *design* isn't quite the same as instructional *authoring*, and it's different still from instructional *delivery*. A *designer* lays out the strategy, and outlines the story that will be told to learners. A designer worries about *how* people will learn, and what *objectives* they're going to be taught. You run around on the Internet today, and it's easy to get the impression that a designer is also worried about which stock photos to use on slides, and what kind of Word template to use; for me, that's an *authoring* job, and it's not something I get into in this book. You'll also see "instructional design" tips like "don't have a boring voice," which for me is very much a *delivery* problem, and so you won't see much of that in this book, either.

I suppose over time "instructional design" has just gotten applied to a wider range of job roles and I didn't notice. That's fine, of course, but I wanted to be clear where *this* book is headed, so that you're not disappointed.

You Can't Solve Learning

You know the biggest problem I have at the gym? Like most humans, I kind of instinctively aim for a more-efficient solution to things. So when my trainer tells me to pick up a few hundred pounds and carry it across the room, I look for a hand truck. Wheels, man. Wheels.

Almost every part of human endeavor is filled with us trying to prevent problems. It's not surprising, given our hardwired fear of failure. Our brains' experience of loss or failure is three times more intense than our experience of gain or success; "a bird in hand is worth two in the bush" is wired right into our DNA, it seems. We dislike failure so much that we try to mitigate and prevent it at every turn.

Consider the employee manual at your job. It's literally chock-full of attempts to pre-solve for problems that have happened in the past. The earliest companies didn't need a manual that told people how to dress or when to be at work, but eventually that became a problem, and so manuals were created to try and prevent those problems. And in most cases, those manuals never 100% prevent the problems they were trying to solve; they just represent a legal defense for firing someone who continued to cause the problems. Municipal ordinances, laws, rules — they're all about trying to pre-solve for a problem. Even the United States Constitution's Bill of Rights is basically a preemptive strike on problems that its authors had experienced and wanted to prevent going forward.

The problem is that people don't *learn* that way. Human beings are simply not wired to ingest a bunch of abstract information and have it suddenly behave who they are and how they behave. Take yourself, or any human, at a very young age: parents tell their kids not to touch the hot pot on the stove, and the kid, at some point, almost inevitably does so. Failing is how we learn.

This is, in fact, the great conundrum of learning. As children, we're relatively less afraid of failure than adults. That's because we haven't learned the downsides of failure, like getting burned by that damn pot. As we grow older, we start to fear failure more and more, because we have a growing lifetime of experience that has proven how painful failure can be. But if we're afraid to fail, and failure it he only way we can learn, then how can we still learn? It's a challenge. Much ink has been spilled over the decades about how adult education is different from child education, and it really all comes down to allaying fear. "Never ask a question of the room and then point at one learner to answer it," I was taught as a new technical trainer, because adults are afraid of "being called on." Adults don't like to look stupid in front of other adults, so they'll often stay quiet, not experiment, and not be as engaged in the class.

Here's one way that "unintentional" instructional designers — people with a life of learning behind them, who find themselves suddenly needing to teach other people — will go wrong. They'll *front-load*. A knowledgeable adult will often break down the task that they're trying to teach, and then reverse-engineer their own learning experience. They'll helpfully try to anticipate every problem they ran into, and construct a narrative that eliminates any chance of those problems happening to the learner. They try to *prevent failure* through what I call "engineered learning." But it doesn't work. That approach just hand-feeds information to someone, without creating strong neural connections that relate to real-world needs and outcomes. Without failure, or at least a dumbed-down failure, learning isn't effective. It's a bit like a vaccine: you can't develop an immunity to a virus without personally experiencing the virus, but that would make you sick. So vaccines (often) contain a synthetic or weakened version of the virus, giving your system a chance to "fail" in a lightweight fashion and develop the immunity you need. Learning needs to be like that: a *vaccine* against failure, but not a *prevention* of failure.

"Unintentional" instructional designers will also try to front-load concepts a lot of the time. "In order to teach you to drive a car, I first need to cover all the rules of the road." That's not *exactly* the best way to learn, though, because of — as we shall explore in this book — the way our brains construct memories and learning. We don't often learn abstract concepts easily, except through rote memorization, which takes longer. We tend to learn — as happens when we fail — by experiencing a problem and then being offered a solution. I'm not suggesting popping the kids behind the wheel and releasing them into the world to see what happens, of course, but you can *simulate* problem scenarios, just as a vaccine *simulates* a virus. For example, show some kids a diagram of a four-way intersection with a car heading each way. Ask, "who gets to go first? How do we make sure nobody crashes?" Let the kids verbally explore their own solutions, and discuss why each might or might not work. If they don't come up with the right answers, meaning *they've failed*, then you can start nudging them toward the right one. By that point, their brains' survival mechanisms will have engaged in an active search for the solution that will prevent a crash, and the eventual correct answer will be more meaningful. The duration of time this experience takes will create more neural "weight" in their brains, and create a memory that, when they encounter that intersection in the real world, will be more relevant and readily accessible.

The problem with this is that *learning takes time*, which is something not all of us are willing to invest. You can *reduce* that time compared to real-world trial-and-error, but you can only reduce it so much. Our brains still need to experience failure, even in proxy form, before a solution will "stick." And we can only learn so much in a given period of time. Learning isn't efficient, and it isn't a problem you can *solve*; it's a process you must *experience*.

And that's what instructional design is all about. It's about understanding the basic cognitive science in how our brains learn, and using that to construct the most efficient learning process *that will still create learning*. It's about understanding the limits of the human brain's ability to effectively absorb new information, and the tricks you can use to make the brain *want* that information. It's about how to get the brain to take new, abstract knowledge, and turn that into practical, real-world application.

And all of *that* is what this book is all about.

Part 1: How We Learn

Understanding how human brains learn is the key to helping them do it better and more easily. In this part, I'll break down some of the yawn-inducing cognitive science into something a bit jazzier and real-world. Much of this chapter's information is draw from *How We Learn: The Surprising Truth About When, Where, and Why It Happens*[1], a book I heartily comment to anyone interested in exploring the topic further.

---

[1]https://www.amazon.com/How-We-Learn-Surprising-Happens/dp/0812984293/ref=sr_1_1?s=books&ie=UTF8&qid=1522363583&sr=1-1&keywords=how+we+learn

Why do We Learn?

The first thing we need to think about is why human brains learn at all. Plenty of creatures on this planet *don't* learn; they respond instinctively do specific stimuli, and there's not much you can do to change that. But for creatures that can learn, and can change their behaviors based on what they learn, there's really only a one reason why:

It helps them survive.

Alligators will "learn" that humans are food providers if humans feed the alligator (sometimes just one feeding will do the trick). Being alligators, they don't always differentiate between "humans bring food" and "humans are food," but you know. Alligators. The point is that most learning, at a very basic biological level, is possible because it's what helps us survive in this cold, cruel world of ours. Brains developed the ability to remember things, and to connect those memories to scenarios, and to process those scenarios, because doing so helps us live longer.

That's why so much instructional design is focused on engaging natural human survival instincts. It's a big part of why the "problem-solution" approach works so well for humans. If our brains can be made to understand that a problem exists, then our brains will seek a solution to that problem. If a solution can then be provided, our brains will tend to lock on to that more readily.

Of course, learning is a lot more complex than just "let's try to outlive the next guy," but our *ability* to learn is rooted in that age-old desire to survive.

What is Learning?

Now we should probably decide what *learning* even means. A gent named Benjamin Bloom, back in the 1950s, came up with a taxonomy for learning, and it remains a useful way to talk about what learning really is. He defined several different *kinds* of learning, and ranked them from fairly easy and low level, up to harder and more high level.

He started with *Remembering*. Basic memorization, in other words. Humans do okay at this. In the brain, memories are formed by connections between neurons. The more neurons that get connected, the stronger and clearer the memory is, and the easier it is to recall. There are a few ways that our brains create stronger memories, and the most basic of those is *repetition*. Forcing us to recall something over and over and over will, over time, create a stronger memory. Memorizing the multiplication tables in school is a great example of this: there's no obvious connection between 3x4 and survival, but the rote memorization process takes advantage of our brains' ability to reinforce memory strength with repetition. That ability is itself a survival mechanism, helping ensure that the most often-encountered facts and memories are available for rapid recall should we need them.

Bloom then moves on to *Comprehension*. This is different than mere remembering; I remember that DNA stands for deoxyribonucleic acid, but I honestly couldn't tell you what that word *means*. Comprehension is when you've remembered something, but also know what it means. You can organize, compare, interpret, explain, and re-state things that you comprehend. I comprehend how a gasoline engine works at a basic level, and I can explain it to you.

Up next is *Applying*. Having come to understand something, you can start applying that something in new situations. You can solve problems, and identify relationships between things. I comprehend how electrical circuits work, and I can apply that comprehension to create new kinds of electrical circuits to solve for specific problems.

Next is *Analyzing*. Once you're able to apply something, you can start breaking it down into its component parts, figure out how those parts relate to each other, and make inferences for new knowledge. Because I understand how oranges help support a healthy diet, I can start to analyze other foods for similarities, and create theories about what other foods might similarly support a heathy diet.

Let's pause for a moment, and think about things you've learned in the past. Too often, formal education often focuses on remembering, asking us to memorize facts but not even worrying if we comprehend them. Comprehension is hard to test, whereas the ability to spit back facts is pretty easy to test. And if testing someone's comprehension is hard, imaging how hard it is to test if someone can perform analysis! But obviously, simply *knowing* something isn't where most of us want to stop learning. We should want to *understand* it, and be able to *use* it in real-world situations.

- This berry is poisonous.
- This berry contains poisons, which when ingested may kill me.
- This berry might kill other forms of life, too. I could maybe kill predators with it.
- If this berry kills, then other plants might also kill. There is probably a family of foods that can kill.
- If I can isolate the commonalities between foods that kill, I may be able to isolate the killing substances, and either neutralize them or harvest them specifically.

That last step is *Synthesizing*, the next step up Bloom's taxonomy. It's the ability to take lots of things that you've analyzed and start building models or discerning patterns.

Finally, there's *Evaluating*. This is the ability to take everything that's come before, and present and defend opinions. You make judgements about information you have, the validity of ideas you're presented with, and so on, based on various criteria. I think we can all agree that, objectively, lots and lots of human beings don't do any kind of evaluating. The need for a site like Snopes.com (which attempts to verify or dispel urban myths), and the frequency with which known-to-be-false stories spread on social media, proves that evaluating is a rarified atmosphere. Evaluation asks us to *question*, and to start from the presumption that whatever we're presented is neither correct nor incorrect, but must instead be proven to be one or the other. That's *hard*, and it creates the possibility for conflict, which most people avoid, because conflict "hurts" and we instinctively tend to avoid things that hurt.

Before you set out to teach anything, you need to decide what level you're trying to achieve. Asking someone to memorize something is easy; explaining it so that they comprehend what they've memorized is similarly straightforward. Helping them learn to apply their new knowledge can be straightforward, too, especially if you're able to present realistic scenarios as you teach.

Moving through to analysis gets tough. Analysis takes a kind of leap, and it often requires a very broad base of learning. Teaching someone how to add and subtract numbers isn't hard; teaching them how a checking account works isn't hard. Teaching someone to balance a checkbook is, on the whole, not terribly hard. Teaching someone to analyze their budget is a big next step. Moving through to synthesis and evaluation is harder yet, because they each require an exponentially larger knowledge base to work from. Those last three — analysis, synthesis, and evaluation — are also like muscles in that, if you never use them, they don't really develop. Kids who aren't taught to question things and to evaluate proofs grow up into adults who often *can't* do those things.

So for better or for worse, most educators tend to aim for application-level learning: knowing facts, understanding them, and being able to apply them in the real world. It's the nature of our brains that make those the low-hanging fruit of education. My point here is that you need to know where you're aiming, instructionally, in order to get there; if you do indeed have a goal of moving someone into those higher three cognitive levels, you need to aim very hard, and very carefully, because they're difficult targets to hit.

Making Memories

The basis of all learning is, of course, *memory*, which is why Remembering sits at the base of Bloom's Taxonomy. So how do memories actually get made in the human brain?

There are three broad areas of the brain that are relevant to memory. The entorhinal cortex, a thin outer layer of tissue, acts as a kind of active filter for incoming content. It's what helps us focus, and choose what to ignore and what to pay attention to. The hippocampus is where memory formation begins, and for those memories the brain decides to keep, the neocortex gets involved to actually store them.

Physically, memories are linked groups of brain cells called *neurons*. When a memory is accessed, that entire group of neurons electrically "fire" at once, recreating sensations, knowledge, and so on. In many cases, the neurons that "store" a memory are the same ones that initially "fired" when we experienced whatever it was for the first time. So by and large, the neurons that "lit up" the first time you tasted chocolate are the same ones "lighting up" right now as you read these words, letting you experience some of that flavor again without actually eating any. The connections between neurons, called *synapses*, actually get thicker the more you use them — almost like a callous building up on skin that's exposed to repeated friction. Thicker synapses are stronger, more readily accessible memories because they can more easily transmit electricity between the neurons they connect.

Memory recall is a tricky beast. It's not at all like opening a file on your computer and reading it, although that's an analogy that springs easily to most people's minds. No, for us, *remembering* is more like asking the brain to photocopy a memory onto a piece of transparent plastic. We then take that plastic, scribble on it, and re-file it on top of the original memory. The very act of remembering can change the underlying memory, which is why police detectives are so cautious about eyewitness reports.

As an instructional designer, this really creates two important takeaways: first, repetition can be an important learning tools, and second, guided repetition can help cement a memory *correctly* without our brains trying to "tweak" the memory. Another takeaway comes from that entorhinal cortex, which actively filters what we're perceiving and potentially remembering: we need to "break through" learners' filters, and make a memory *important* to them, or it won't "stick." And we need to do that judiciously, because brains simply aren't designed to remember every little thing. Imagine if yours tried to actively remember every teensy little detail of your daily life! You'd be awash in mostly useless memories, and rapidly find yourself unable to function.

Numerous studies — and I won't bore you with the cognitive science details here, but you'll find them in the Additional Reading section at the end of this book — have defined some limits on how much new information the average brain can assimilate in a given sitting, and about how many hours a single learning session can practically last. We know that there's a *forgetting curve* of sorts, a span of time over which new memories are likely to become less strong. However, we also know that letting a memory fade a bit, before later reinforcing it, can actually create a stronger memory in the end game. There's a definite science to memory, and it forms the basis of some of the guidelines I'll introduce you to later.

The way the brain stores memories also gives us a clue for how to make better memories more quickly. A single memory isn't just one neuron floating alone in our gray matter; it's a bunch of them, all connected in a network via synapses. *Connected.* Our brains are story makers, and they seek patterns and relationships automatically. New information is more likely to be retained if it can immediately connect to an existing network of neurons, especially ones that already have strong, thick synaptic connections. This is the power of analogies, where we take something already familiar to the learner, and adroitly connect something new to it. Imagine that you need to hang a new piece of art — are you more likely to be successful hanging it on an existing, sturdy wall, or attempting to hang it on a recently-strung sheet of paper?

Current cognitive science suggests that all memories have two "strengths:" a storage strength, and a retrieval strength. Storage strength is simply a measure of how well we learned something, and we can increase that through repetition and by actually using the memory. Storage strength, the theory goes, can grow, but never decrease. We never *lose* memories, although they may, through disuse, become disconnected from the neurons we *do* use, making those memories essentially irretrievable. That's the retrieval strength: a measure of how easily a memory can be brought to mind. This also increases with use, but it drops of rapidly if the memory isn't being used. So while our brains are in theory full of everything we've ever learned, we really can only access a subset of it any any given moment. Retrieval strength rebuilds quickly, though. For a memory with a strong storage strength, a quick reminder can often bring it back to full, roaring life after years of disuse.

So: as instructional designers, we want to help our learners build memories that have a high storage strength, and as much as possible connect them to existing, strong memories. That provides the best chance for a high retrieval strength, or at least the ability to quickly re-build retrieval strength in the future.

But first we need to break through that damn entorhinal cortex.

Cracking the Filter

There are a couple of reasons kids learn more readily than adults. One is simple survival: in a rush to not wind up on some apex predator's plate, younger brains rapidly absorb everything they can and start constructing stories. But another reason is the world a kid lives in. It's relatively less "full" than an adult's world, meaning the entorhinal cortex doesn't need to filter stuff quite so aggressively. We tend to put kids into formal learning environments that actively minimize distractions. As adults, though, we've got to get through our morning commute, worry about the bills, keep junior's soccer schedule in mind, and do our actual day-to-day job. Our filters kick in hardcore. Never forget that the job of the brain filter is *beneficial*, because if we let our brains start forming high-strength memories out of everything we experience, we'd quickly lose the ability to navigate our own memories. It's not that our brains would "fill up," it's that the slightest provocation would retrieve far more memories than we'd be able to deal with. Our filters are designed to *protect* us, by not creating strong memories out of anything not deemed important right then.

Learning, then, requires us to make a strong enough case to those filters to let strong new memories be created. It's a bit like auditioning for a television competition like *American Idol*. Before you get in front of the four main judges and a TV camera, you first have to get through the phalanx of interns in several phases of screening. They're the filters, making sure that the "real" judges only get the best of the best (and the occasional too-bad-to-be-true performer, just to keep the viewers engaged). So if we're going to create strong new memories in our learners, we've got to put on our best singing voice and really impress those interns.

Brains, for better or for worse, are biased. Tell a Pepsi lover that you're going to discuss the health advantages of Coke, and you've already lost half the battle. So you have to start by finding common ground with your learners, and that's often done through story-telling. By casting them in the central role of your narrative, and by starting the story at a time and place they're already familiar with, you engage the brain's biases, rather than working against them. This is nominally why instructors are advised to go 'round the room on the first day of class and "do introductions." You're meant to get a feel for where your learners are starting, so that you can frame your story appropriately.

Familiar analogies are another way to break the filter. When you start with what is obviously a story of sorts, you're setting the filter at ease. "I clearly don't need to remember this," the filter says, as it relaxes and grabs a glass of water. If your analogy invokes existing memories in learners, firing up existing neurons, the filter can remain relaxed. If you then add a bit of information to that existing neural network, just tacking on a small new neuron or two to the existing collection, the filter's less likely to sit up and take notice. This is just a new coloring on existing information. If that existing information already had a strong synaptic network, then it's already been deemed "important," and so attaching new information won't raise any red flags. In this way, we can sneak new bits into the brain, bypassing the filter.

The point here is that, for adult learners, *you need to clearly make the incoming information relevant to them* or their filter will just try to block it all out. We'll look at several techniques for doing so, but keep in mind that the whole reason behind it all is to get that filter's permission to start creating new memories.

Memory to Application

So how does the brain move from mere memorization through comprehension and into application, and how can we as instructional designers assist it on that journey?

Let's first address what cognitive science people mean by *application*. I've worked for years in the technology industry, and "training classes" often consist of a lecture, which is meant to cover the operational theory and "why" of a technology, followed by hands-on labs. These labs are *meant* to reinforce the lecture, and to create a stronger memory by having the learner actually use what they've just learned. But too often, these labs are basically long, numbered lists of *exactly* what to do. This is literally *training*, in the way that you'd train a dog or a dolphin; it's not *application*. Learners aren't being taught something and then tossed out on their own to start using it; there's no actual cognitive connection between the lecture and the lists of tasks you can simply follow *without thinking about it*. These types of classes often skip the *comprehension* step, and without comprehension, there can be no true application.

Comprehension happens when the brain can bring together multiple pieces of information that it has memorized, and start relating those pieces of information to each other. Comprehension is understanding the *why* of a topic, and that often requires a broader set of background information. For the human brain, comprehension usually requires us to have a story, of sorts, around the topic that we're learning. That story helps us draw all of the necessary facts together into a sort of pattern, or narrative. With comprehension, we're not just reciting facts we've memorized; we're able to place those facts into a sensible context.

A key indicator for comprehension is a learner's ability to restate the topic in their own words, explaining it to someone

else, and to ideally be able to create their own analogies to explain that topic.

To aid the learner in achieving true comprehension, we need to go beyond just teaching them some end fact that we want them to know. It's not enough to say, "the US Constitution was created over the course of several months in the 1770s, and was largely a compromise between various different political goals held by the delegates to the Constitutional Congress." That's a fact, but it doesn't get into the details of those compromises, those varying political goals, or any of the other context of the situation. To really get a learner to *comprehend* that topic, we'd need to spend a lot more time providing historical context, relevant anecdotes, and so on. Achieving comprehension *takes a lot more time* than simply teaching facts, and it's one reason that we, as instructional designers, start to become constrained in how much we can actually teach in a given period of time.

Moving learners to *application* level learning takes even more time. To continue with the Constitutional example, we'd want learners to be able to suggest changes that they might make if the Constitution had to be rewritten from scratch. Not changes to the text, but changes to the process that we'd just taught them about. We'd ask them to identify "holes" in the narrative we'd taught, getting them to look for missing facts. Getting a learner to that point involves a lot more discussion, and an even broader background of information to work from.

To switch to a somewhat simpler analogy, let's say that I, as an instructional designer, was asked to design some instructional tool that taught you, the learner, how to build a cabinet with shelves and drawers.

- If my goal was simply to achieve remembering, then I'd give you precise plans, some basic information on the tools required, and call it a day. You'd only be able to build the exact cabinet I gave you plans for, though.

- If my goal was to achieve comprehension, then I'd have to do a little more work to explain the engineering that goes into a cabinet. How wide can a shelf or drawer be? How much weight can they bear? How might different joining techniques increase strength or stability? This would enable you to more fully understand *why* cabinets are built like they are, and explain the process to someone else.
- If my goal was to achieve application, then I'd likely go even deeper into the engineering and possible variations. We might discuss the different kinds of materials involved, for example, and I'd want you to be able to build cabinets for a variety of situations.

Training, again in the sense of what you'd do with a dog or a dolphin, often requires little more than remembering. But to make a human being self-sufficient in a task, you need to move them through to application. They need to be able to perform a task on their own, with little guidance, and deal with at least common variations or alternate scenarios.

None of this is impossible, but far too often instructional designers set out with an arbitrary list of things they want to teach in a given period of time, and don't think about how heavy a burden they're taking on if actual comprehension and application is the goal.

And let's be clear: sometimes, remembering *is all you need to achieve.* When I worked on F-14 Tomcat jets, we had a big room filled with manuals on how to put one together. Like, literally hundreds of manuals for every possible part and system on the aircraft. These were mainly step-by-step task lists, and provided you had a basic understanding of how to use the tools involved, you could probably get the job done. You'd never know *why* that particular kind of bolt was used in that particular spot, and you'd never be able to make any kind of substitutions, but that wasn't the goal. As a mechanic, I didn't *need* to know, and I wasn't *allowed* to make any alternate decisions, and so simply *remembering* the steps involved was sufficient. And, because the manuals were largely designed to remember *for me*, very little teaching was, in theory, required.

My education on F-14s actually *did* go further. I had plenty of classroom time to learn the theory of operation — the "why" and "when" — of the aircraft. The intent was to take me through comprehension and into some degree of application so that, in theory, I could work on a battle-damaged aircraft and make decisions about how to get it in the air quickly, if not optimally. That education took *time*, though. Four years of it, to be precise; if all the Navy had wanted was a monkey to put the planes together, they probably could have accomplished that in four months or less. Every step of the cognitive ladder takes an exponentially longer amount of time to accomplish.

Takeaways

Here, in convenient bullet-list form, are some of the main things I hope you picked up from this Part:

- Memory is the foundation of learning, but it isn't the whole of it.
- Memories can be reinforced through repetition, but they're *best* and most strongly enforced through *use*.
- Comprehending something means you can explain it to someone else, in your own words.
- Applying something means you also know *when* and *why* to apply it, not just *how*.
- You can only teach so much in a day, and teaching to apply takes a lot of time.
- Adults have a lot of "learning filters," so before you can teach, you first need to create a strong case for why what you're teaching is applicable to them.
- One good way to get adults "on your side" in learning is to create a story that puts them in the central role, and that takes them on a journey.

That last bullet is what we'll dive into next.

Part 2: Telling a Story

Our brains are *story makers*. We try to fit everything we learn into the larger pattern and narrative of our lives, and so one of the best ways to help our brains learn more easily is to provide a ready-made story. There's a real art to this, and it's perhaps the most important Part of this book.

Why Stories Work

Other than oddball stories (ABC's *How to Get Away with Murder* springs to mind) where you start with the end of the story, and then quickly get "THREE WEEKS EARLIER" and work through the story backwards, most stories are *sequential*. Actually, simply saying that something is sequential isn't useful, because even a story that's told backwards can be sequential; it's just in the opposite order. The "right" order, for our brains, is based on our built-in understanding of *causality*. That is, we're accustomed to seeing a cause first, and then its effect. We drop a glass of water, *then* the glass shatters, *then* the floor is wet. When we witness the entire story, we know why the floor is wet and the glass is broken.

Our brains are *so* hardwired for this kind of understanding that it's almost impossible to get our brains to stop doing it, even when we know they're drawing the wrong conclusions. And when we don't see the *cause* of something, we can make some pretty egregious mistakes in analyzing the *effects*. Ever walk into the kitchen, see something spilled on the floor, and then immediately assume the kid/pet/ghost was the cause? You don't *know* they are, but your brain has seen them be the cause often enough that it just assumes it's the cause this time, too. Show someone a wrecked car and their brains will immediately start filling in the *start* of the story, based on their past experiences. Ask ten people in a crowd what happened, and you'll get a bunch of different answers, based on their past experiences. Some may temporize their theory with words like "maybe," but very few, you'll find, will come right out and admit they don't know. Our brains *need* a complete story, and they'll happily make one up where none exists. For proof, look no further than the many myths our ancient ancestors to created to explain how we all got on this planet in the first place.

So as a learning technique, stories work because *that's how our brains work*. Give a hammer to someone who has never seen a hammer before, tell them, "this will hurt your thumb," and they won't really *learn* anything. They haven't seen a cause, let alone an effect; they haven't been told a *story*. You may have thought you were saving them some time by getting straight to the point, but our brains aren't wired for time-saving. They're wired to learn from experiences, and stories embody those experiences.

The Elements of a Good Story

Once we accept the story-based nature of our brains' learning system, we need to start looking at what the brain needs in a story to make that story effective. Really, you only have to look at some of your culture's oldest children's stories â€" fairy tales, that is â€" to see the best elements boiled down to their absolute essence.

First, a story needs to be *relatable* right from the outset. If the learner can't relate to the story's basic premise, then you'll lose them immediately. That's why good teachers talk about making the learner the *hero* of the story. Put learners into a position they've experienced before, or can easily imagine themselves in, as a starting point. This is where you create common ground with your learner, and it requires that you first have a clear, unambiguous definition of who your audience is. In *Hansel and Gretel*, two children start with a horrible parent abandoning them because they eat too much. This is something most children can instinctively relate to, because fear of abandonment is baked into our brains (when teaching children, who have so little experience of their own, you often have to start with these built-in fears and biases to find "common ground"). With adult learning, we almost always start with familiar analogies (in my industry of information technology, the analogies always seem to involve cars, which are a near-universal experience in most parts of the world). This need to find common ground as a starting point *will* limit how much you can teach in a given time period. If you're trying to teach quantum physics to a teenager, your "common ground" is going to be pretty far away from the end goal, and that goal might in fact not be achievable in the time you've got.

Second, a story needs to follow a clear cause-and-effect pattern.

Hansel collected pebbles, used them to lay a trail, and used that trail to get himself and Gretel home after their mother tried to abandon them the first time. Their mother then prevented them from leaving the house until the next attempt, so that they could not gather more pebbles. This is a clear cause-and-effect sequence. Nowhere in the story are there "spoilers," right? You didn't read, "Hansel collected pebbles, but he knew that would only work for one attempt. Next time he figured he'd use a slice of bread." You've lost the causality of the story with the foreshadowing. I try to avoid foreshadowing whenever possible; I don't tell students what they're going to learn in the future, and instead focus on what they're learning *right now*. Foreshadowing causes the brain to build a kind of expectation-placeholder, which does nothing to help the *current* learning task.

Third, a story needs to expose the learners to problems, then the solution, and right into the next problem. This is one of the most difficult tasks in building a storyline, because you ideally want to address *one* problem at a time, let the learner absorb the fact that it's a problem, and then address *just* that problem. The solution should lead as naturally as possible into the *next* problem, keeping the brain hungry for a steady diet of solutions. That's how we learn. We're not *removing* the experience of the problems themselves, just shortcutting it a bit. "Don't you hate walking into a dark room? And you don't always want to put a lamp right next to the door, right? So you might put a lamp on the far side of the room. But then you'd still have to walk through a dark room to reach it! But, we could put an electrical outlet over there, and wire it back to a light switch right by the door! But, we might have a hard time remembering which outlet is controlled by the switch, which means we could accidentally plug a clock into it and end up switching the clock off. But, we could install that outlet upside-down, so it was visually apparent it was different somehow." Problem, solution, problem, solution. So long as each problem is one the learner can see and relate to, the sequence doesn't necessarily have to be the exact one they'd run across if they were just figuring this out on their own.

Fourth, the story needs to have a definite ending, and you need to call it out. "And so now you'll never have to walk through a dark room again!" The ending needs to connect right back to the problem statement that started the story, subtly informing the learner that the entire story is now part of their "common ground," familiar place. The ending tells the brain that the story is concluded, and that the brain can now start processing the story into long-term memory.

Fifth, the story must continually connect to learners' existing experiences, often through familiar analogies. Introduce only one new concept or idea at a time, and immediately relate it to the learner through a sub-story or analogy. This helps new concepts immediately connect to strong neural networks in the learner's brains, giving them a better chance of synthesizing the new material.

Sixth and finally, understand the limits of human learning and retention. Our experiences each day are kept in short-term memory, which has a finite amount of storage in each person. It isn't until that night, when we go to bed, that the brain reviews the day's events, rebuilds neural networks, and expands those networks to include new experiences. If you exceed what I call the Daily Learning Capacity, learners won't retain what you've taught, and you'll have to start over the next day. Hansel and Gretel taught us just a couple of moral lessons in their one story together; they didn't try to aim for any more than that. The actual amount a person can learn in a given period of time varies pretty drastically. Well-constructed stories that are adjacent to existing, strong experiences can often teach more than something more esoteric or novel, for example. In my *Month of Lunches* series, for example, I mandated no more than one hour's worth of learning (based on the average adult reading speed, that dictated chapter lengths) per day. That places some strong limits on how much is taught at once, and lets the learner's brain process the information overnight before taking on new information the next day.

Recall and Relate

Don't forget that repetition is our brains' way of figuring out what is most important to our survival. Things we experience more often are, by the brain's definition, more relevant, and more worthy of a strong neural network. Things we're forced to recall develop a stronger "recall" ability in our brains, and develop stronger synaptic connections with other information and experiences.

For example, many of the websites you probably use on a day to day basis are big and complex. Once you start drilling down through pages, it's often easy to forget where you came from, unless you just use your browser's "Back" button a lot. You've probably noticed that some sites will, near the top of each page, try to show you the "path" you've taken. It's usually a series of links, like this:

```
1   Home > Your Account > Privacy Controls > Who Can See Yo\
2   ur Data
```

In the world of web design, this element is literally called a *breadcrumb*, recalling poor Hansel and Gretel, who tried to leave a trail of breadcrumbs the second time their mother abandoned them in the first. Of course, on the web, there are no birds to eat our breadcrumbs, so we can always find our way Home.

See what I did, there? I started with the familiar shared experience of complex web sites. I pointed out a solution, and then connected it with information you'd learned earlier. Your brain, whether you realize it or not, had a big "OMG!" moment. *Breadcrumbs* will now forever hold a stronger importance in your brain, because that visceral story of Hansel and Gretel now has a real-world, familiar application that solves a problem you've experienced personally.

This recall-and-relate technique is what lets good teachers conduct full-day learning sessions. If you think of each day as a series of stories, with each story forcing learners to recall from previous stories and relate to the current one, then you start forcing the brain to prioritize information on-the-fly. That night, even after a long day of learning, the synapses connecting the most important facts are already flagged for strengthening. Of course, you have to take great care to identify the most important things you want learners to learn and retain, and make *those* the subject of your recall-and-relate moments.

And that's where the real instructional design challenge happens. You need to find the one, central theme of your overall story arc, and that it like an immense steel girder. From that girder, you can hang your individual stories. That girder is what you keep coming back to, though. It's where you want the strongest synaptic thread in your learners' brains, and you rely on its recall strength to help learners recall the other, smaller stories that make up the learning experience. Take the *Star Wars* saga as an example. Its main thread, throughout, was the Skywalker family: Anakin, Luke and Leia, and eventually Leia's son Ben. Numerous other stories attached to that main arc, and we can easily recall moments with Jabba, Emperor Palpatine, Padma, and more, because they're all connected to that central Skywalker theme. That central theme is so strong that we can now imagine other stories that have no direct connection to the Skywalkers, such as the stories told in *Rogue One* and *Solo*. We "learned" each of those stories in just a couple of hours apiece, and most of us can easily recall the sequence and major events of each one through their connection to the overall backbone.

This is where the true art of instructional design lies. So how do you find the Skywalker Saga in whatever it is you need to teach?

Start by defining who your learner *is* at the *Phantom Menace* stage of your story. The beginning. What do they know? What have they experienced? What common ground will you have with them? Then define who they are at the end of *Episode IX*. How are they different? What have they become? What can they do now, that they couldn't do in the beginning? Then start analyzing the gap between those two extremes. Sometime it's easiest to start with the end state, and work backwards. *OK, to get to this endpoint, the last thing they're going to need to learn is Z. In order to learn Z, I'm going to have to teach them Y. But Y isn't going to be possible unless they first know X.* And so on. Each of those steps form the smaller stories you'll tell, creating the granular learning experiences that take just a short period of time apiece. They're the episodes in your saga, if you will. And as you do that analysis, look for the common threads that will connect those episodes. *Create* a storyline where each episode picks up from a thread of the previous episode. Look for that strong backbone that defines the entire arc, and construct your analogies and other learning aids around that backbone.

It's not easy, but few things really worth doing are.

Storytelling Checklist

Here's a quick summary of this Part, which you can use to evaluate the stories you construct for your learners:

1. Start on common ground. Make the learner the "hero" of the story by starting in a familiar, relatable situation.
2. Stick with a linear, cause-and-effect storyline. Avoid foreshadowing and let each portion of the story unfold in sequence.
3. Create a story that introduces problems the learner can relate to, and then a sensible solution for each problem, which should lead right into the next problem, and solution, and so on.
4. Make a definitive ending statement that connects back to the story's initial problem statement, marking the end of the story and cueing the brain to begin long-term archival.
5. Constantly relate new story points to learners' existing experiences, often through analogy.
6. Carefully limit how many new things you try to teach in one sitting.
7. Use recall-and-relate to construct multi-part stories, forcing the brain to recall key bits and connect them to the current story. This strengthens the memory and lets you tell longer, connected stories in a single learning session.

Part 3: Nine Tricks for Learning

Humans have some interesting built-in behaviors that you can judiciously exploit to help them learn. These come with some pretty heavy-duty caveats, which we'll also explore, but used in the right place and in the right measure, these are invaluable instructional aids.

1. Lather, Rinse, Repeat

Repetition is important... but only when it's the student that's doing the repetition.

Anyone who's been to a Disney park can tell you how well repetition works. It's a small world after all, it's a small world after all...

Instructors and instructional designers have long known about the value of repetition. Keep telling someone something and eventually they'll remember it. The concept is put to good use with primary education in K-12, and even in college: students take notes (repetition), do homework (repetition), and recite facts on demand (repetition, repetition, repetition).

Unfortunately, most of those techniques aren't available to adult educators. Adult learners who are aggressive note-takers aren't engaging in repetition, they're just missing the lecture or demonstration. The goal becomes copying everything down, not absorbing it, and their notes lack the nuances and subtleties of the original delivery, making the notes a poor way to actually learn the material. Adult learners simply won't do homework, so that's out. We also don't call on individual learners in class for fear of embarrassing them, so verbal quizzing is limited to throwing out questions to the group and waiting for the "smart guy" in class to answer.

Adult educators still recognize the value of repetition, so lacking these other mechanisms they tend to just say the same thing over and over. It's all they've got. So they end up droning, repeating themselves ad nauseum and losing the attention of their students.

All of which misses the whole point of this chapter.

The famous phrase on the bottle of shampoo says, "lather, rinse, repeat." Of those three tasks, which are the most important?

Lather and rinse. That's what actually washes your hair. Do you really need to repeat? Probably not. I never do, and my hair stays pretty clean.

That is the whole point of this chapter. Yes, repetition can be important — but what's more important is physically taking action. Let me give you an example.

I often teach technical courses where the courseware has the instructor perform some kind of product demonstration. There's usually a mix of lecture and demonstration, in which the lecture explains why or how something works, and then the demonstration shows how it works. That's a form of lightweight repetition, and the general consensus is that it works well to reinforce key concepts and show the student how to do something. After a while of doing that, students go into a hands-on lab where they often perform the same tasks that were just demonstrated — more repetition.

What I found through some experimentation is that the demonstrations are almost completely ineffective when used in that manner. Adults have to do some odd context-switching when you move from talking to them to showing them something. The amount of time needed for that context-switch isn't long, but it isn't zero, and they end up not absorbing most of the demonstration, as well as missing a few key points when you switch back to lecture. It's like putting someone in the passenger seat of your car, driving them to a location they've never been before, and explaining something to them the whole way. They're not going to learn the route you took and be able to get to that destination on their own.

As an experiment, I started skipping demos where I knew the same tasks were in the upcoming lab. I stuck with the lecture, and then dumped students, "unprepared" into the guided lab. They were much more successful. They stumbled a bit here and there, but frankly they'd stumbled the same way when I'd just demonstrated how to do whatever the task was. The demonstration added nothing, and dropping it had zero impact apart from saving us time and keeping students' minds more on-track. After the lab, students were more confident of performing their tasks – I could give them an ad-hoc exercise related to the lab, and they'd be able to complete it more quickly and more surely.

Doing something is how adults learn.

There's another technology I'm well-known for, and I'm probably one of the more experienced instructors for that technology. One of my personal quirks is that, when I teach it, I don't use slide decks or perform the normal lecture-style presentation. My "lecture" is almost 100% demonstration, coupled with me waving my hands around a lot while talking. Students like the approach, because it's more interactive. Also because, quite honestly, staring at slides is boring. But I discovered that my approach had some flaws. Students don't learn from demonstration. There's too many brain components working at the same time for actual comprehension to kick in for most folks. What's happening on the screen up front is completely detached from students' existence. Their eyeballs and brain have to pick out the bits on the screen that are moving, relate that to some hazy goal they've been told, all while memorizing task sequences that don't yet have any context for them.

Cooking shows do this all the time. You watch the TV cook prepare some beautiful dish, all the while waxing poetic about the quality of the butter, that time in Napa they had this same dish in a wonderful restaurant, and how you have to be careful not to use too much oil or you'll burn the pan. The facts are flying fast and furious, and they don't always precisely match what's presented to your visual cortex. Nobody learns to cook by watching TV. At best, they get a recipe idea, which they then have to look upon the channel's Website to actually try.

Outright demonstration isn't always an effective learning tool, even when it's not being used simply for repetition. Students have to do something, themselves, before they'll actually grasp something.

I've since modified my approach. Knowing that the lab — the student's hands-on "lather, rinse" activity — is the important bit, I've shortened both lecture and demonstration sequences. I talk and/or demo for as little as possible, and focus on giving students the information they can't self-discover, such as background concepts. I teach one thing, and then try to get them to a lab where they can practice that one thing as quickly as possible.

What about repetition?

It's in the labs. I design my hands-on activities so that students not only practice what I just taught them, but also re-visit tasks that they learned earlier in the class. I don't re-teach those things, but I make students re-practice them frequently. By the end of the class, the things they've repeated the most, as you might expect, "stick" really well.

And therein lies the instructional design challenge. There are really two principles here, neither of which seems very revolutionary, but both of which can be pretty hard to actually achieve:

- Your class' most important skills need to be introduced as soon as possible, so that students will have the most amount of repetition with them throughout the class. Everything you teach one day 1 gets repeated every other day.
- Your class has to use a very carefully designed outline, so that you're constantly building. Chapter 1 has to teach something that will be reused in Chapters 2, 3, 4, and so on. That's where the repetition comes from.

These two simple facts drive one of the most important instructional design activities in the world — one that a lot of course authors skip or don't do properly: triage.

Look, you can't teach someone everything about a complex topic in a single class. You just can't. You have to pick and choose. Let's say you're teaching them about driving a car. You decide, early on, to teach them how to change the oil in the car. How often are you going to repeat that in subsequent lessons? Probably never — which means you either shouldn't be teaching it, or you should be teaching it last. If it doesn't naturally lend itself to repetition throughout the class, then it isn't a core concept, and it either belongs at the end or it doesn't belong in the class at all.

These two principles really do force you, as a designer, to identify core content. You can only teach an adult about 3-4 new things an hour before their brains stop absorbing. You know the course's earliest hours have to start with things that can be repeated in every upcoming hour. You know you can't teach something that depends upon something else that you haven't yet taught. The course outline almost writes itself.

You will wind up discarding material — not teaching them at all — that you thought were absolutely crucial. That's a natural side effect of properly applying this chapter's principle. If something doesn't bear constant repeating, and isn't something students can actually perform hands-on, right then, then the material gets shifted later and later in the course. It's entirely probably some material will get shifted right out of the course altogether... and that means the material wasn't so crucial, after all.

Not coincidentally, this approach helps you better define class prerequisites. As you start to build your outline, you may find that you want to shift early material "forward." In other words, you'll identify key concepts. "I can't teach them how to boil water until I teach them how to turn on the stove. But I don't want to go that basic – I want to shift 'turn on the stove' to a prerequisite. They have to show up knowing that skill." That's a legitimate design decision — so long as it's documented and communicated to students. It's something that the instructor should review right at the start of class, so unqualified students can at least know they're unqualified. Whether they choose to address the issue is their own problem.

Let's look at a straightforward example of this entire approach, with the goal of teaching someone to put up the framing for a house. We'll presume that the prospective student isn't designing the framing, but that they're simply being asked to physically implement someone else's design. They start with a pile of lumber, boxes of nails, and some basic tools. I've actually seen short courses on this topic, and they'll often start like this:

- The purpose of framing
- Structural loads and framing standards
- Building a basic wall
- Raising and bracing the wall
- Connecting walls
- Framing doors and windows

Those first two bullets shouldn't be there. I hate teaching abstract concepts on their own, because it forces students to queue up material in their brains for later application, something the adult mind does not like to do. Ask yourself, "how many times will students have to repeat an exercise on the purpose of framing?" The answer is zero, and that means the item should either be moved down the list, or off the list.

This outline misses some basic points. What's the proper way to hammer nails into the wood? How should the wood be cut? Those are key skills that will be repeated in every upcoming lesson, and those skills should either be taught first, or clearly listed as prerequisites.

The rest of the outline may be in pretty good shape. "Building a basic wall" seems to be something you'd repeat: you'll build one before raising one, you'll build one before connecting one, and you'll build one as part of framing in a window or door. Raising and bracing seems like something you'd repeat a lot, too, so that earns a spot early on in the class.

This example brings up an important practical point, which is the balance between the need for hands-on repetition and the logistical limitations on how long you've got to teach. In an ideal world, you might structure your class like this:

- Nailing and Sawing
- Building a basic wall

  - Sawing the wood
  - Nailing the pieces together
- Raising and bracing the wall

  - Sawing the wood
  - Nailing the pieces together
  - Raising the wall
  - Bracing the wall
- Connecting walls

  - Sawing the wood
  - Nailing the pieces together
  - Raising the wall
  - Bracing the wall
  - Connecting the wall

In other words, each new section repeats everything that has come before. That's a learning ideal, but it's rarely practical. Due purely to time considerations, you'll have to forego a certain amount of hands-on repetition. Some courses do this by continually building on previous work: you build the basic wall, then you raise and brace that same wall, then you connect that same wall to an existing wall, and so on. That's zero repetition, and while you might have to go that route in order to teach the necessary objectives in the time allowed, it's far from ideal.

The ideal is probably somewhere in the middle. Build a wall. Raise and brace it. Build a new wall, raise and brace it, and connect it to the first one. Core skills, taught early, are getting repetition with that approach — you're building two walls. But you're not starting from scratch every single time.

The overall theme of this chapter is to teach as little as possible before letting students practice something themselves. Work in small steps, through a carefully planned progression that permits explicit and implicit repetition of core skills. Give students pre-constructed "starting points" only as a way of meeting time restrictions, but don't completely eliminate hands-on repetition. The skills you teach earliest, and repeat the most often, are the ones students will truly take home with them, so strategize carefully and triage the material as you must.

And never forget that it's the lathering and rinsing that washes your hair.

Give students plenty of opportunity to encounter and re-encounter the most important items you are teaching. Repetition is important, but students must actively repeat, not simply be repetitively lectured.

2. Don't Pre-Order — Deliver

Foreshadowing is fine for Shakespeare. You're not Shakespeare.

My single biggest pet peeve is a class where the instructor mentions something, but doesn't immediately cover it — "we'll cover that later."

Now, while you're learning to care for camels, you should also know about their one magical super-power, that can make you rich beyond your wildest dreams. But we'll cover that later.

Every single time an instructor does that, at least half the class is thinking, no, cover it now!! I'm actually okay with "we'll cover it later" in response to a question. If a student asks something, and you know you'll get to it, then by all means let them know you'll get to it. You'll eliminate a possible tangent, satisfy their immediate curiosity, and if you're a really good instructor you'll acknowledge them again when you actually do get to whatever it was.

I'm not okay with "we'll cover it later" being brought out in any other way. Sequence your material so that you don't have dependencies on future material. That is, until it's time to talk about something all the way through, don't talk about it at all.

Foreshadowing creates a cognitive "to do" list in some students' brains. They start trying to create connections to material that you haven't even covered yet, and they start building this list of expectations for what's coming up. None of that serves any useful learning purpose. If it's coming up, students don't need to know that. They'll be there when it comes up, right?

Worse, foreshadowing immediately sidetracks the brain from whatever you are covering right at that moment.

Let's explore this from an instructional design perspective. The goal of instructional design is to create learning materials that do the best possible job of teaching some topic. In order to do a good job at instructional design, you have to keep in mind how your learners' brains are reacting to what you're doing to them. Humans — especially adults — have funny brain stuff going on all the time, and a ton of instructional designers just completely ignore it.

For example, let's take the concept of stating a module's (or chapter's) objectives up front. I'm not a fan. Yes, you absolutely need to give your learner some idea of what you're about to cover, but as I wrote in this book's first chapter, your title should do that. "Riding a Horse Without Falling Off" is a pretty clear explanation of what a chapter is going to cover. Immediately following that with a list of objectives?

- Mounting the horse
- Sitting in the saddle
- Holding the reins
- Walking the horse
- Moving into a trot

Blah, blah blah. The learner doesn't care. Those are what instructional designers call enabling objectives, meaning they're things you have to cover in order to deliver on the promise of the chapter title. Ultimately, students only care if you deliver on that promise — they don't necessarily need an outline of how you're going to get there.

Here's a perfect, real-world example that any traveler has experienced. "Hello, this is Captain Dave. Welcome to flight 1234, headed for Philadelphia. On the way, we'll be passing over the Rocky Mountains, and you'll be able to get a view of Denver off the left side of the plane. We'll be turning South a bit to avoid some weather patterns over the Central Plains, and turning North again around Arkansas."

Seriously? Am I supposed to remember that? Should I have brought a map? Look, Dave, I paid you to get me to Philly. How you go about it is your problem, and I don't need a rundown.

The point is that presenting that huge list of objectives is the same thing. It isn't actionable information — the student can't do anything with that list right then. But adult brains will grab on to that list because we love lists. Checklists especially. So now the brain will start trying to make sure we hit all the items on the list. It isn't setting itself up to be receptive to those items, it's just looking for them. Instead of learning, it's trying to complete a collection.

Then you hit it with the "we'll cover that later." "Oh, and along the way, folks, we're going to be testing out a new APU in the airplane. That's an important piece of equipment, but I'll tell you about it later." Crap. Now my brain wants to hang on to that, and I'm going to fret about what the stupid APU is, and why can't you either just tell me now or shut up about it until the time comes?

That's the key lesson of this chapter: If you're not ready to talk about it right now, then it isn't important right now, so just keep it a secret so that I can focus on whatever is important right now. My brain is working pretty hard already in your class (or book, or whatever), so let's just avoid giving it a bunch of future expectations, okay?

Following this rule requires the most careful possible sequencing of material in a class or book. So much so, that I routinely refuse to deliver pieces of a work until the whole thing is done. I'll be in Chapter 5, ready to write about "x," when I realize I have to cover "v" and "w" first, and that I haven't done so. So I have to restructure, rewrite a bit, and move on. "Ugh, if I bring this up now, I'm going to have to cover it very lightly, and then touch on it in more depth later. That being the case, maybe I should just not cover it at all until I can do it all the way. Later." For example, "steering a car is really easy, but it's similar in many ways to steering a motorcycle. We haven't talked about motorcycles yet, but for now you just need to know that they have two wheels. We'll get to the rest later." This is one very common use of foreshadowing — pulling in some example, but not wanting to get off on a tangent and fully discuss it right then. Use a different example. Don't set up the "to-do" item that foreshadowing creates.

Now, that said, you can cover something lightly, and then circle back to it for more complete coverage later. Just don't tell students you're going to circle back later. Just briefly cover whatever you're going to cover, and leave it at that. Students don't need to know you'll be covering the same topic in more depth later — they'll know when you get there. Again, if a student asks, it's okay to put them off — "yes, we'll cover that in a bit" — but you don't need to make a big deal of it.

So: sequencing. It's the magic that makes a good class into an awesome class. Always present material so one topic leads naturally into the next, without having to "refer ahead."

Minimize distractions by not foreshadowing information. Sequence material so that students only have to digest a single stream of information, rather than building a "buffer" of "what's coming up next."

3. Experience the Problem Before Offering the Solution

Until you care, you just don't care.

Humans are often described as tool-using animals. That description, however, missed the point. Sure, we make and use tools all the time — but why? We typically make tools to enhance our own physical abilities, or to accomplish things we can't physically accomplish ourselves. In other words, we make tools to solve problems. The hammer wasn't invented until someone got tired of banging rocks on things. In other words, we don't just go around inventing things for no purpose — we invent things to solve problems.

It's stunning how often this fact gets missed in learning materials, but there's a reason: kids are sponges.

This is going to take a minute to explain, so bear with me.

Kids tend to learn without needing reasons. In other words, you can teach them abstract concepts, not really explain why they need to know that thing, and kids' spongy little brains will soak it right up. You absolutely shouldn't teach that way, but you can get away with it. Elementary school math is a perfect example, as was the horrible — and now largely discontinued — practice of making kids diagram sentences. We teach kids to add one and one, but we never really both telling them why. In other words, we give them the solution in advance of the problem. Sometimes, it's just easier to do so — can you imagine, for example, trying to explain the concepts of bookkeeping or sales tax or some other real-world mathematical task to a second grader, just so you can start talking about addition and subtraction? Ugh. One and one is two, little Johnny. Write it down.

Unfortunately, that elementary school experience is where most adults learn how to teach. We get a little locked into that approach early on, and because most people don't think about how they learn, they don't question the approach. Just show someone how to do something, and they'll learn it. Sadly, adult brains are less absorbent than kids'. Adult brains, as I've written in previous chapters, don't want to learn as much. The brain is busier with day-to-day nonsense, and before it learns something it sits down and asks itself, "seriously, do I need this to survive, or can I ignore it?" Humans don't have conscious control over that behavior — try to show something to our brains that we don't need to eat and breathe, and it just slides off. The more abstract the concept, the less likely our brains will seriously care. You can point your eyes and ears at something for as long as you want, but your brain just won't soak it up unless there's a reason.

Now, the way most training materials try to combat this is by giving you a reason. "Frying pans get hot," a book might tell you, "and so you have to use a potholder when you pick one up off of the stove." Problem and solution in one neat sentence. Except that telling your brain to care is not the same as making it actually care. Remember, this triage behavior of your brain — wherein it only pays attention to things that it thinks are important — isn't conscious. You can't bypass the brain by reasoning with it. So every time a course does the typical problem-solution statement approach, the brain often doesn't pay attention, and the material doesn't stick.

You know what makes something stick? Experience. Put your hand onto a hot frying pan and your brain will assuredly remember the pot holder trick the next time. You can't present the problem to the brain. The brain must experience the problem — but once it does, it will seek out the solution, and it will by God remember that solution.

Experiences don't need to result in physical pain, though — any "failure" situation will do. Simply frustration at not being able to accomplish a task. Deep curiosity about how to do something better. Anything, really, that makes the brain want a solution will work.

This is why narrative sequencing is so vitally important in adult learning materials. In the previous chapter, I wrote that I use sequencing to ensure I'm not foreshadowing material; I don't introduce something until I'm ready to talk about it more or less in full. That's still an important rule, but a companion rule is that your sequencing also needs to allow for natural, self-discovered segues from unit to unit (whether those units are book chapters, class modules, or something else).

For example, suppose you have a book chapter that discusses cooking basics. You explain how to select an appropriate pot, how to fill it with water, and perhaps how much salt to add to the water (we're cooking pasta, here). You wrap up the chapter by explaining that the pasta will only cook if the water is hot... creating the obvious question of how to make the water hot. The next chapter covers boiling the water, including safety precautions, how to watch for when the water is boiling, and so forth. Of course, once it's boiling, you need to dunk the pasta in it... which is the problem covered in the next chapter. That's obviously a lightweight example, but the idea is to sequence learning material so that each unit ends in an obvious problem statement — one the student's brain can immediately agree with, and one that the student's brain may in fact have already been asking.

Some important take-aways, here:

- You aren't giving the learner a problem statement — you're asking them a question, which lets them form their own internal problem statement. "But how can we get the water hot?" gets their brain in agreement. Simply stating the problem doesn't accomplish the same mental agreement.

- You have to sequence material really, really carefully, so that you can flow from one instructional objective to the next by means of a series of learner questions. You do have to "set up" the learner for those questions, but it's important for your material to make the questions natural and obvious. Yes, you're leading the witness — that's the point.

This can be difficult. It requires a lot of communication skill, writing ability, and in live classes a lot of presentation ability. Instructors are mentally geared to answer questions, not to ask them — and certainly not to leave questions hanging, which is exactly what you have to do.

Let me offer a more realistic example. I often teach about a product called Windows PowerShell. One of the things you can do with PowerShell is construct computer commands. When covering that topic, I'll start students with a fairly basic command that uses some hardcoded piece of information, like a computer name. Students invariably ask, "okay, but how can I make that computer name easy to change, if someone wants to run the command on a different computer?" Well, that's the next chapter. Then it's, "how can I require them to enter a computer name when they run the command?" Next chapter. "How can I document the fact that they have to enter a computer name, and provide examples of proper command use?" Next chapter.

You'll never be able to set up a sequence like this until you've taught the material a few times. Teaching lets you try a sequence, and lets you pay attention to students' natural mental progression. By observing that, you can re-sequence the material so that you're getting the questions in students' heads, and presenting material in a natural order. That's why some of the best instructional books are written by people who've taught that same material to a live class. A teacher who's got a good delivery sequence for the classroom is a teacher that's had a bad sequence a few times, and who has worked through and re-sequenced the material.

I used to own ferrets. The thing about ferrets is that they're latrine animals, which means they tend to do their business in the same spot. Unlike cats, they won't seek out a place to make their toilet — they just kinda pick a place they feel comfortable with. That means you don't get to decide where the litter pan goes. Instead, you must observe where the ferret backs his little butt into a corner, and plop a litter pan in that spot. You're observing the creature's natural tendencies, and leveraging that to get what you want. You aren't going to re-train the ferret, I promise. But you can still get it pooping in a pan, if you play along with its brain.

That's pretty much how you need to sequence your instructional material. Come up with a sequence that you think works, then try it — ideally with a live class — and observe where the students' brains seem to wander. Don't try and wrest those brains onto a course of your own choosing. Sequence your material so that you're satisfying the brain's own wandering. Obviously, different students will "wander" in slightly different directions, so you'll need to sort of look for large trends and go with those. You'll also need to set up your students' brains.

For example, when I talk about building PowerShell commands, I start — as I wrote previously — with a simple command that has a static computer name. In my materials, I emphasize that. "This command only targets the computer named FRED. If you decide you want to target a different computer, you have to open up the text file containing the command, and you have to go to the computer name, and you have to type in a new computer name. Then you have to save the file, and go back into PowerShell, and then you can run the new file." By this point, every student brain in the room is thinking, "what a pain in the butt that is." I've made them feel the pain. They can picture themselves doing what I described, and they don't like it. "Isn't there any way to have it just prompt me for the name?" someone will quickly ask. Next chapter. Without my belaboring the point, some students may have wanted to know how to add a password to the command, and others might have been wondering what was for lunch that day. By setting them up, I got them wandering in a pretty natural direction — some of them were already wondering how to make the computer name easily changeable — and I got more of them wandering in that same direction.

I don't want to understate how hard this is. Most authors can fully understand the desire to sequence material in a logical fashion for presentation. I'm going to show you this, because you need it to know this other thing, which you need to know before that last thing. I call that "dependency sequencing," and it's a pretty obvious design consideration. But after you come up with that sequence, you need to make sure that it's also presenting the material in a natural order. Before you teach B, you need to teach A — but when teaching A, are students led to an obvious, natural question that leads them to be curious about B? Do they want — nay, do they need — B by the time you get there? If not, you're either going to have to re-sequence your material, or you're going to have to re-write your discussion on A to make the path to B much more obvious, natural, and desirable to students' brains.

If you don't make them want the next topic, their brains won't care. If their brains don't care, they won't learn it effectively. Period.

Help students embrace new information by first helping them experience the problem that the new information solves. Explaining the problem in advance isn't the same as experiencing it.

4. Make Real-World Actually Real-World

This chapter is going to earn me some evil looks, I know. It's because I'm about to take a time-honored instructional design trick and tell you not to do it. It's a trick developed and espoused mostly by people with one or more PhDs hanging on their wall. They're probably smarter than me. But they're wrong on this one. I've actually tested it, and I'm right-right-right.

Instructional designers and authors love to write scenarios. They'll even go so far as to call them real-world scenarios. In many instances, these scenarios are a required element when you're writing a course for someone who has a pattern or model. For example, when I've written courses for Microsoft, every hands-on lab absolutely must, full-stop-and-no-debate, be introduced with a "real-world scenario."

You are an administrator for Consoto ["Contoso" is one of the most common fake company names in Microsoft's courses]. You and your colleagues frequently create new user accounts in the company's Active Directory domain. This process takes several minutes per user. The new user information is provided to you by the Personnel department in the form of a CSV file. You want to automate the new user creation process by using Windows PowerShell.

First of all, nearly anyone who's been through a couple of these courses sees one of these scenarios and just skips it. It's like getting a new Blu-Ray player. You flip open the manual, there's a page of electrical safety warnings blah blah blah, nevermind-I'll-just-start-plugging-things-in.

The intent of these scenarios is laudable enough. The idea is to give the student something that they can relate to. "Here's why you want to learn this." That falls neatly in line with what I wrote in the previous chapter, right? Wrong. These scenarios miss the bit where you can't tell someone's brain why it cares. The student's brain needs to construct reasons for caring — it can't be told. "You're an administrator for Contoso." No I'm not. "You frequently create new user accounts." No, I don't. We have another team for that. YOU DON'T KNOW MY LIFE!

And that's really what it boils down to. An an author, you can't lump all of your students into a single pile. In order for a scenario to work — in order for it to create context for a conversation, and in order for it to give the learner something to relate to — the scenario must be something the student recognizes. There is no way in the world you can write something real-world that every learner will relate to.

When I first started teaching a particular automation technology, I needed to show some real-world examples in my demonstrations. I was teaching people who worked in a Microsoft-based technology environment, so I had a lot of things to choose from. I could have chosen messaging, for example, because every environment has e-mail, right? But messaging systems typically have dedicated administrators, in all but the smallest environments, and I knew I'd have students who weren't even allowed to touch the messaging system except as an e-mail user. So I figured I'd use Microsoft's authentication service, Active Directory, for my examples. Every Microsoft-centric environment uses Active Directory, and it touches nearly every Microsoft-branded business technology component. Whether you need to send an e-mail, open a shared document, or print a file, you're using Active Directory. Every student in my class should know what a user account was, and how one was made, and so creating new user accounts would be a good example. Boy, was I wrong. Literally two-thirds of the students in my class would immediately go glassy-eyed the minute I started talking about creating user accounts. "What's the matter?" I'd ask. "I don't really do that in my company," they'd say. "Well sure, but you know it has to be done, right? You know this exists?" They'd shrug. It was abstract for them. What I was showing them had no bearing on their personal, daily lives, so they didn't care. You can't make the brain care. It cares about stuff that affects it. It ignores the rest.

And that's why these fakey scenarios fail. If you're going to show me how to change the toner in a copy machine, I'll care if that's something I do as part of my job. If I don't do that as part of my job, no amount of storytelling is going to make me care. I'm just going to sit and wait until you get to something I care about. And if I do change toner as part of my job, I sure as heck don't need some little story to get my attention. I know what the problems are already from personal experience. So the scenario is either useless or redundant.

The next argument is usually, "well, it might not be useful, and it might be redundant, but it doesn't hurt to have it in there."

Disagree.

When I was a kid, we'd sometimes go out to a restaurant for dinner. I can't count the number of times Mom would say something like, "don't fill up on bread and water before they bring out our food." Mother, bread is food. Tasty food. And you're telling me not to drink water? What kind of parent are you, anyway? Now, of course, I realize that what she was saying was more like, "bread has practically no nutritive value, and water has zero, but they take up room. Your little tummy only has so much room, and if you fill it up with those, you'll be hungry again by the time we get home, and I am not making you a sandwich."

I am a firm believer that the human brain can only take so much input in a given period of time, and there's quite a bit of casual experience and formal research to back me up on that. What I refuse to do is give my students bread and water while I've got such large entrees already set to come out. Sure, most of my students will skip the scenarios and get right to the main course — but some will read the stupid things. The scenarios will not enrich the learning experience, but for some students the scenarios will take up brain space. Precious space I'm going to need for actual learning. One reason I'm a successful instructor — and I gauge success by student retention and application, not by whether or not students like me — is because I'm concise. My business partner and I named our company "Concentrated Tech" because we know technical people value concise information. Even a single wasted word, one that adds no value to the conversation, is painful to me. Thus, I hate fakey scenarios. They add nothing. They are waste.

What's funny, for me, is that you never see fakey scenarios anywhere else. We don't use them in K-12 education. They're rare in undergraduate courses. The assumption in both cases, I suppose, is that you're there to learn, and you'll just learn without a little story that's supposed to make you feel "connected" to the material. You don't see scenarios in any other kind of communication aimed at adults, either. Commercials — which focus on delivering a concise message in an extremely short period of time — spend time extolling product benefits and the like. There may be a story behind the commercial, but you don't have to get a preparatory paragraph first. Newspaper and magazine articles — which also aim to be concise — don't start with a scenario. So where did we get the idea that scenarios are necessary?

Scenarios aren't bad in all forms of learning. Some people get a little carried away. For example, I saw a quote at an instructional design seminar: "Creating thought-provoking scenarios stretch the learner's imagination and help them journey through varied emotions until they reach their learning peaks." Zoinks. That's a lot to lay on the shoulders of a little story. But the general idea behind scenarios is to help a learner imagine themselves in a particular situation. If they can do so, the reasoning goes, then they'll "feel the problem," and be more receptive for the solution. It's basically the approach I outlined in the previous chapter, except that I think it's a false presumption. For one, a lot of adult learners don't have a great deal of imagination. And, particularly in vocational-style training for a particular profession, learners aren't showing up to learn about what other people might need, they want to find solutions for their day to day problems. If you have to give me a narrative that helps me imagine myself in someone else's shoes, then go find that someone else and teach them your class. I came to class looking for something else, and if you're going to teach it, I won't need to imagine myself in that situation. I'm in that situation, for real, every day.

This is why I tend to advocate for an approach that puts the learner in a hands-on situation that lets them experience the pain (or whatever), instead of telling them a story where they imagine themselves in a situation. For example, let's say that you're not especially interested in being a garbage collector, but for some reason I need to teach you about more efficient trashcan design. I could start with a scenario: "You're a trash collector. Your manager tells you that you need to cover more houses in a smaller amount of time, but existing garbage can design requires you to spend almost 90 seconds at each house. You would like to design a more efficient trashcan."

Got that in your head? Can you smell the trash, and feel your muscles burning as you lift those unwieldy cans? No?

Another approach would be to walk you outside and have you empty a few inefficiently designed garbage cans. "Here are ten cans. You've got five minutes to empty them. Go." Afterwards, we could discuss — as a class — what made the task harder, and how a different can design might make it easier.

Which approach do you think would be more effective?

I'll conclude with a final appeal for practical engagement over scenarios. I'm sure you work for, or have worked for, or at least know someone who works for, an organization where managers have made some pretty stupid decisions. Blindingly, obviously bad decisions. And I'm sure that, upon observing those decisions, you've thought to yourself, "wow, if that person had ever worked in this job, they'd know how stupid that is." Exactly. That's what happens when you ask someone to imagine themselves in a situation, versus putting them in that situation. You might tell a story to a manager about your job, but it'll never be as concrete or as valuable as if they just do your job for an hour.

So as you design your instructional materials, try to avoid an approach that relies heavily on scenarios and imagination. You're adding to the student's reading load, and you're not adding a lot of value to the class. Scenarios don't teach much, and they don't really get the learner's brain to "buy off" on the upcoming instruction. They're a distraction, and an ineffective one in most instances.

Artificial scenarios won't resonate with every student, and they create a distraction. Create an overarching narrative that involves students experiencing problems, and they'll embrace the solution without needing a scenario.

Now... all that said, there *is* a time and a place for *actually real-world* scenarios. In fact, one of my oldest math class memories, going back to probably 7th grade or so, is when our teacher passed on photocopied pages with fake, blank checks on them. We had to go through an exercise of writing checks, keeping the checkbook register up to date, and later balancing the checkbook. *That*, friends, is real-world. It wasn't a made-up scenario that I can't relate to; it's really-real, just like real life. So *that's* when "scenarios" can work: when they're not fake, when they contain a genuine experience, and when the scenario is a *part* of that experience.

5. Shut Up

Instructors talk too much.

And, along the same lines, authors write too much.

Really, I should just end this chapter there. But I'm being paid by the word (not really), so let's expand on that. When I've taught a class a few times, or written on a subject a few times, I find myself becoming more and more concise. I eliminate stray material, because frankly the extraneous stuff isn't what my students came for. My most recent book was under 600 pages and my publisher was annoyed, because they'd priced the book for 800 pages and had to adjust. But concise is better. Write less. Talk less. Force yourself to be concise.

I think this comes down to objectives. If you haven't decided up front exactly — in a good amount of detail — what you're going to teach, then you're going to teach too much. Perfect example: a colleague was using one of my In a Month of Lunches books to deliver an in-house class. After his first day, he tweeted, "don't get outside the chapter! you will not finish!"

This happens to a lot of instructors and writers, and it happens all the time. Instructors — good ones, at least — are enthusiastic about their topics. They want to share. They want to share as much as possible. They cram in little extra tips, tidbits, and trivia. They become a veritable firehose of information, blasting into an unsuspecting crowd.

It's too much.

Humans simply can't digest that much — something I touched on in this book's first chapter. As I wrote there, you need to decide in advance exactly what you need to teach. What skills are you going to enable? What is the absolute minimum amount of information you must impart in order to achieve those goals? Can you reasonably and effectively do so in the time available? You're an expert in your topic, but you amassed that expertise over a period of, what, months? Years? You can't impart it all in a single class, or a single book. It's too much. So, once you've narrowed down your learning content into the absolute minimum, focus on also minimizing the number of words it takes to impart that knowledge.

An example: I've had to teach people how indexes work in Microsoft SQL Server. I've worked with that product for over a decade, and I know how indexes work, but I hadn't really taught the subject at the time. So I watched a few other instructors, most of whom followed the material in Microsoft's official curriculum for SQL Server. The average index explanation took over an hour. Ugh. I didn't have an hour, and watching those other guys, quite frankly, made me bored (I don't have the attention span to sit in a class myself). So I started looking at the material more carefully, narrowing down exactly what you needed to know, and trying to cut down on the sheer verbiage. A picture, I've been told, is worth a few hundred words at least, and so I created some diagrams to help explain some of the stickier bits. The first time I taught the class, I took about 45 minutes to cover that subject. On subsequent deliveries I pared it down to 25-30 minutes, which is kind of a magic delivery time number for me. I took the time to question my students carefully, and to re-question them on subsequent days, to see how much they'd retained. They retained a lot — and most of them could explain the topic back to me, or to the other students, on request. As an experiment in a later class (never take a class with me unless you're okay being an unwitting guinea pig), I reverted to a longer, almost 60-minute delivery — and retention fell way off.

In a previous chapter I mentioned a magazine editor I worked with, Keith Ward. He's the one who taught me that learning to write an 800-word column, instead of a 2,000-word article, would make me a better writer. He was right. Concise is the watchword of training.

Let's use an analogy: imagine that you like chocolate truffles. Imagine, too, that you can choose between one of two boxes. The first box contains ten truffles. The second box contains ten truffles and 5,000 ping pong balls, wrapped in foil just like the truffles. Which box would you prefer? Probably the one that's more concise — that contains just what you want, with no extras. Right?

Which is why this is perhaps the shortest chapter in this book.

Ask yourself what you can safely eliminate from your delivery while still meeting your learning objectives. Deliver as little material as possible to accomplish your goal, and don't overreach your goal. Just because you have extra time or pages doesn't mean you must use it all.

6. Be Profound

Boring instructors go to hell when they die. Possibly before they die.

I'm probably most well-known for teaching a Microsoft product called Windows PowerShell. PowerShell is an odd product. It's intended for administrators, but it uses a very different approach to administration than many of them grew up with, and there's been a lot of resistance, by some folks. The problem is, Microsoft is really moving toward that approach, and folks are putting their career in serious jeopardy by not getting on board. It's like making steam-powered cars after the invention of the gas engine — you're just in denial. So I came up with a little catchphrase, which has become a mildly famous proverb in the Microsoft world: "Learn PowerShell, or learn to say, 'would you like fries with that?'" It's a deliberately demeaning, dramatic statement intended to elicit a chuckle, but also to make a very important point. It's easy to remember — like a good song lyric, it bears repeating and becomes a meme unto itself.

There's a component in PowerShell that produces textual output, which actually flies in the face of what the shell is and does. That component has some specific uses, but people tend to stumble across it and use it inappropriately. This "Write-Host" command, as its called, actually creates a hurdle for learning the product, because it gets you moving in a direction that makes just about everything harder than it needs to be. So I'm also mildly famous for the saying, "every time someone uses Write-Host, God kills a puppy." There are t-shirts, even. The statement isn't even entirely true, because as I've noted there are legitimate uses for the command. But it's a humorous, dramatic — profound — statement that sticks with you. After hearing it, folks think twice before they set down that direction, which was the goal. Later in the class (or book), I'll expand the discussion and talk about when the command is good and when it's inappropriate, but the profound statement sets the stage and creates a lasting impression.

The point is that over-the-top, profound statements are an excellent learning tool, provided you use them sparingly, and only in places where a memory would otherwise be difficult to create. The more abstract the concept, the more likely a dramatic, possibly humorous statement will be effective.

Another component of PowerShell is its built-in help — essentially, its operating manual. The help file has its own complex syntax involving way too much punctuation. For example:

```
Do-Something [-computername <string[]>]
```

It's a bit abstract, and that makes it hard to remember. The item in <angle> brackets tells me that the computer name must be a string of characters, and the [] indicates that I can provide multiple names if I want. The outer [brackets] indicate that the whole thing is option — I don't have to provide a computer name.

Explaining this in a live class is especially hard, because — unlike in a book — students can't "rewind" and review something you've just said. You end up trying to rely on repetition alone to drive the point home, and that isn't always effective with everyone. An instructor I know has used profundity to make everything easier to remember. His approach to "profound" isn't a catchphrase, though — it's almost pantomime.

"What's the parameter name?" he'll ask. "Computer name!" the class responds. "HOW DO YOU KNOW?" he'll shout. "THE DASH!" they all say, and every student holds up one hand in a horizontal position, miming the hyphen that precedes parameter name. "What kind of data does it take?" he'll ask next. "Strings!" they answer. "HOW DO YOU KNOW?" And the students, to a person, hold up their hands in "angle bracket" positions, and cry out, "cha-hooah-hooahs!" which is the name the instructor gave to angle brackets.

"Can it take more than one?" he asks last. "YES!" they yell, holding up their hands in [] square brackets. It's a delivery technique I can't quite bring myself to steal, but damn is it effective. He also leverages repetition, because every new command he shows them involves a repeat performance, complete with pantomime. The hand motions, the repetition, the performance, and the nonsense "chahooahhooah" name all combine to make for a memorable delivery of an abstract, difficult-to-remember concept. He does all this on the first day of class, and what's impressive is that one days 2, 3, and beyond, students are still playing along, and getting it. When they get stuck in a lab, all he has to do is hold up the "cha-hooah-hooah" hand sign, and the student says, "ah, right!" and they're off and running. Profound. Effective.

If you think about it, most of the mnemonics we're given as kids, to help with rote memorization, are also profundities. "Superman Hates Eating Onions" is ridiculous, but memorable when it comes to the names of Great Lakes (Superior, Michigan, Heron, Erie, Ontario, I think). "Man Very Early Made Jars Sitting Up Neatly, Period" helped me remember the names of the planets, nonsensical as it is.

You do have to time your profundities carefully. I find that I get about two per day, max, before they stop being affected — and I use that limit as I'm sequencing material to make sure the over-the-top statements are appropriately spaced. If there's an easier, or less dramatic, way to help students remember something, I'll explain that. And, because profundities aren't always 100% accurate, I do have to take the time to explain the underlying meaning and any exceptions. I'll never give that explanation in close proximity to the profundity, though, because doing so diminishes the impact, which was the whole point of the thing.

"Profound" also doesn't universally mean "silly." Sure, there are some silly things — "cha-hooah-hooah" — that can be used in an impactful way, but they work in large part due to contrast. In other words, they work because the rest of your delivery is more serious and professional, so that one silly thing sticks out... profoundly.

Profound also works in books, although obviously you lose the opportunity to use pantomime and other physical delivery tricks. You become limited to phrases, and it is a lot harder to make a phrase stand out from all the other phrases around it. I tend to use italics a lot for emphasis, as you've seen, and boldface is obviously an option. However, in many kinds of writing those elements are reserved for other things — boldface is often used, in technical books, to refer to user interface elements ("click the OK button"). So you have to get a bit more creative to make your profound statements really stand out. I've found that, rather than using visual styling, I get more impact by building those profound statements into a short story. Just a paragraph, maybe three or four sentences; I'm still acutely aware of wasting space. But because I don't tell many stories in my writing, when I do tell one, it stands out for just that reason.

So why does "profound" actually work? As with most of what I've written in this book, it works because of the way our brains work. Humans tend to build their worldview around markers and milestones. We celebrate annual events like birthdays, we navigate largely based on landmarks ("turn right at the post office"), we often shortcut rote memorization by using mnemonics. Making profound statements not only provide contrast with the rest of an instructional delivery, but they tap into our brains' desire for landmarks. When they're big, memorable statements, our brains grab on and tend to not let go easily.

Make an impact — but do so judiciously. People — aside from cable news anchors — can't take constant shock-and-awe, but a well-timed (and humorous) jab can make something really stick.

7. And Now for the Top Ten

You only need to remember three things from this chapter.

You only have to look at modern media to see that people are natural collectors. Hoarders, even, although most of us try to control our acquisitive urges. Video games offer badges and achievements, scavenger hunts remain a popular pastime for kids and adults, collectors of all kinds invest considerable time and money completing their collections.

We can leverage that behavior in instructional design. Now, most instructional designers will agree because they've always been attracted to numbered lists. They'll tell you that people work well with numbered lists, especially when those lists describe some sequence of tasks that the learner must perform. That's all true, but it isn't what I'm talking about. A numbered list doesn't encourage collecting. It's like giving someone a complete set of postage stamps — there's no actual collection activity. Collecting requires the collector to expend effort to obtain each item in the collection, and there's an implied period of time between each acquisition. During that interval, the brain savors its most recent acquisition, and greedily anticipates the next one. What you have to do is set that up properly, by telling the brain — that is, the learner — that a collection opportunity is coming up. You clearly communicate how many items will be collected, and you highlight each collection opportunity. Learners won't consciously perceive all of this, in most cases, but their brains definitely will.

For example, one topic that I've written on has a number of features designed to help people learn to use the product. Specifically, there are three of those features. I typically have an instructional unit dedicated to each of those features, and so I start with an overarching narrative like, "there are three discoverability commands that you need to know — and if these three are the only commands you remember from this entire course, then you'll be fine." Then, as I introduce each element, I call attention to it: "this is the second of the three commands I told you about. Remember that the first was named 'Help,' and this one is called..." and so on. That allows me to use repetition — I get to repeat the name of each command as I introduce new ones — as well as engage the collector portion of learners' brains.

That approach also does something else for me. While brains will be (subconsciously) eager to collect when there's a known quantity of items to acquire, learners' brains can get a bit (consciously) anxious when there's an unknown number of items. That's especially true when you're teaching an unfamiliar topic. A lot of adult learner anxiety comes from a simple fear of the unknown: "I don't know how much there is to learn, I don't know what it's going to involve, and I don't know if I can do it." It's like getting onto a thrill ride in a theme park, without being able to see it first. In that case, the anxiety is part of the attraction; in class you want to avoid it. So my approach tells students that there are (for example) three important things coming up — and if they can learn those three, everything else is just icing. The brain immediately decides, "ah, three things I can definitely handle, and it's safe to ignore the rest." Now obviously, that's not entirely true — the rest of the class is hardly "optional." But because I sequence the material so that these three critical pieces get covered up front, I can continually reinforce their use throughout the class. Additional learning items almost take the form of practical exercises in using the three critical things, so while they're not optional, I'm not entirely untruthful when I say that those three things are the main bits the learner needs to remember.

Some authors have argued that stating a list of learning objectives will trigger the "scavenger hunt" reflex, but I don't entirely agree. In any course you write, you're going to have a variety of objectives, none of which are of the same "flavor." In other words, a class on car maintenance might involve changing oil, changing wiper blades, adding gasoline, and so on. But those are all very different activities. You can't necessarily point to them and call them a collection. What you could do, perhaps, is say, "you're going to learn to change three kinds of fluid," and then get the student to "collect" those similar skills. However... what's the point? The student knows they're going to learn those things, because presumably they were listed in a course abstract or outline, right? You don't have to trick the student into remembering the objectives, because for the most part you don't care if they actually remember the objectives themselves. You don't need the student to recite a list of things they're going to learn. So I don't rely on objective to create "collections" for my students.

Enabling skills are what you want students to collect. "Now, to be really successful as a car mechanic, you're going to need to know how to use a variety of tools. But there are really only four types of tool that you need to worry about — if you can get those four, the rest will be easy." You wouldn't list "use a crescent wrench" as a course objective, because that isn't a useful job skill. The job skill might be "change the oil," with the crescent wrench being a means to that end. But by using "tools" as a collection, you can get students' brains to start looking for those things. You reassure them that they can handle what you're about to throw at them ("...only four types of tool..."), and you give yourself an opportunity for important repetition ("the third tool is a socket wrench — it performs the same basic task as the crescent wrench and adjustable wrench you've already learned about, but...").

Don't overuse collections. Like any leveraged behavior, it works best when engaged as a strategic element in a class. Most people, for example, only collect one or two kinds of things. Maybe it's comic books, maybe its stamps, maybe its petrified bugs — but it's rare for a person to engage in "collector" activity in a number of different things. That's party because a collection represents a kind of "to-do" list to the brain, and it'll get anxious if it has too many "to-dos" stacked up. By saving the "collector behavior" for the most crucial information in your course, you'll help the brain focus. It does mean that you, as an instructional designer and author, need to really triage your information and decide what's truly crucial. I always ask myself, "if I could only teach someone three to five things in this topic, what things would give me the biggest bang for my buck?" I might, for example, decide to only teach the student about crescent wrenches, and to downgrade my focus on similar tools like adjustable wrenches or sockets. Those are nice, to be sure, but I can get most of the job done with a basic crescent wrench, and downgrading the time spent on other wrenches lets me involve a couple of other critical components, like screwdrivers and hammers.

Remember that you can't teach everything. Every course will always omit something that would be great for the student to know — and most courses will have to, by sheer practical necessity, omit several great things. I spend more time doing triage on my material to make sure I can do a fantastic job teaching what will fit into the course's allotted time. Focusing on "collections" of information helps me do that. "Man, there are ten things I'd really like to show them — but I'm going to cut that list down to five. What five things are the most awesome, the most useful, and the most important?"

Get your students' brains ready to collect information by presenting them with small collections to acquire. Try to sequence your material to introduce items in the collection over a short period of time, maximizing the brain's anticipation and satisfaction cycles.

8. You've Got 30 Minutes to Make This Real

Nothing cements knowledge like using it — but you have to get there quickly.

Human beings are doers. We're noteworthy on our planet for being one of very few species to create and use tools, but the fact that we're "tool users" is really a symptom of the fact that we do things. Our brains learn best by doing. Engaging our brains and bodies in something makes it real for us, and really makes new skills concrete.

Practical experience also serves another crucial learning goal: the opportunity to fail. After all, no matter how well-written a course, and no matter how great an instructor's explanations, and no matter how wonderful the demonstrations, when you do it yourself for the first time, you're likely to make a mistake. Our brains really learn well when we make a mistake, find out what we did wrong, and then correct ourselves on a subsequent attempt. Whether it's baking a cake, assembling a machine, programming a computer, or even drafting a last will and testament, it's the opportunity to try something, fail, and then succeed that makes for effective learning.

The problem I find with most courses and books is that they don't get students into hands-on experience quickly enough. Our brains are pretty terribly at queuing up information for later use; until we've used something, our brains are thinking, "this isn't useful, so I don't want to remember it." Using new knowledge gives your brain a context for it, and a reason to hang on to it. Too many authors and instructors forget that fact.

For example, suppose you bought a cookbook, and suppose that it started with a lengthy discourse on the origin of wheat as a food item, going into deep detail on how grains are harvested, milled, and packaged. Yawn. Most readers would skip all that and get to the recipes, right? In fact, why even include that information? Well, the information is useful, and it is relevant. Knowing how wheat is milled gives you a greater understanding of how different flours are used in different recipes, for example. But your brain doesn't want to queue up all that background information for later use — it wants to start doing stuff.

Once you accept the maxim that students should get no more than about 30 minutes of education before they have a practical experience, you force yourself to sequence material a bit differently. Background material that just isn't relevant gets dropped. Conceptual information that is relevant gets introduced as concisely as possible, to save time, and tends to be taught "just in time," right when the student needs to know it. In my cookbook example, you might dive right into a recipe for cake, and learn that a specific kind of flour is preferred for light, airy cakes, and learn a bit about the milling that makes the flour right for that task. The next recipe might be for bread, and might briefly discuss why that requires a flour that's been milled a bit differently. The discussion on how grain is actually harvested gets dropped, because while it's interesting, it doesn't really lead to better baking.

The idea of dropping information is a controversial one, and it's probably the one principle in this book that I argue about the most when I speak to instructors, authors, and instructional designers. Instructors want to be a fire hose of information. They want to cram data and facts into the course — and into students' heads. They believe students value "hardcore" learning where only the fittest survive. They speak of "crash courses" and other filled-to-overflowing approaches. The problem is, students don't retain much of that information. Students tend to retain only what they've been able to practice and experience, on their own, within about 30 minutes of learning it. Jamming more information into a course does not make it more valuable. You cannot teach it all in one sitting. Instead, you have to — and I've probably used this word in every chapter up to this one, so I might as well use it again — triage your information. You have to pick the most important, impactful, and reusable information and teach that. You have to get students using it quickly, or you might as well have skipped it — because without rapid progression to practical experience, the material will be lost anyway.

My courses tend to consist of short "sprints" of lecture, coupled with demonstrations as appropriate. A sprint might be 30 minutes, but it might just be 10. I teach one thing, and then get the students using it. When possible, I try to build on that one thing through subsequent sprints, and give students a chance to repeatedly practice each new skill through a series of hands-on experiences. Those hands-on periods might also be short; while I've certainly written labs designed for multiple hours, I've also designed lab experiences that take just 15 minutes. The course becomes a smooth flow of learn-try-learn-try-learn-try.

Of course, in a book you might think the whole "hands-on experience" thing is a little tough to achieve. After all, unlike an instructor-led class, books don't have labs and such, right? Wrong! In fact, a hallmark of my In a Month of Lunches series of books is that they do instruct students to "Try it Now" throughout each chapter, and most chapters conclude with a hands-on exercise. The chapters are written so that most adult readers can get through the text in 30-45 minutes, leading them directly to a self-paced "lab."

So how can you tighten course material to just a short "sprint?" Obviously, eliminating extraneous information is key. You can still provide "further reading" references so that students have a jumping-off point for future, self-paced education and exploration, but tighten your course material to the bare minimum needed to accomplish your ultimate learning objectives. I literally sit and go through every single sentence in a course, once it's written, and ask myself how each one contributes to the stated objectives of the course.

Second, eliminate extraneous delivery. For example, I would rather a student do something on their own than demonstrate that same thing to them, so I'll frequently cut out demonstrations so that I can get students into a hands-on experience more quickly. I'll often limit my demonstrations to those that provide basic orientation. In a cooking class, for example, I'd quickly run through the tools the student was about to use, so that they could recognize and use them. I might demonstrate a whisking technique, but I wouldn't demonstrate an entire recipe. Yes, students will probably get something wrong on their first hands-on attempt — but that's the point. So long as you can provide guidance to help them self-correct, then they'll learn.

I avoid, as much as possible, trivia. For example, in a class on car maintenance, students need to be aware that engine oil gets dirty, and needs to be changed. They might need to know a few of the reasons why oil gets dirty, so that they can make good decisions about how often to change the oil — more frequently in dirtier environments, for example. They do not necessarily need to have an extensive education on the negative effects of leaving dirty oil in the engine. Yes, that's useful information, and it might well offer students more incentive to pay attention to oil changes. But you could probably provide that with a simple statement of fact: "dirty engine oil can cause major damage to the engine." Done. So really evaluate what you, as a course author or designer, think is important, versus what really is important. And, try to deliver the important material in the most concise fashion possible. When a statement or two can convey the information, there's no reason to construct a multimedia presentation that takes four times as long to deliver. Less is more.

What if you've got some information to deliver that doesn't lend itself to any kind of practical experience? I'll boldly suggest that such a thing is not possible. If people can't do something with it, then they probably don't need to know it. Unless your course goal is to simply have people memorize facts (and what a boring course that would likely be), everything we know leads to hands-on experience. The nature of that experience might not always be obvious, so you may have to get creative and really think about it. For example, you might think that a course on family legal planning might not have a lot of practical experience opportunities — but isn't the whole point of such a course so that the learner can review, or perhaps write, legal documents? So that's the practical experience. Even when the "hands-on" material doesn't involve anything more than reading, it's a practical application of what was just taught — and so it helps cement things in the brain.

As I've written earlier, I always construct my courses by starting with the ultimate learning objectives, and I like to write those as things you would do. "After completing this course, you will be able to do the following" kind of phrasing. I then design hands-on experiences around those objectives, because hands-on — doing things — is how we learn best. The course material then simply sets students up for the hands-on experiences. Because the hands-on bits embody what I wanted to teach, I don't need to teach anything that isn't used in those practical experiences. The material practically writes itself from that point.

Sequence material so that students are introduced to a very small number of items, and then immediately given a chance to put those to use. Avoid any lengthy instructional sequence that doesn't lead to hands-on experience. The Part on Constructionism, coming up, really lends itself to this small-batch learning approach.

9. Don't be Afraid to Be Glossy

An automobile is just like a horse-drawn carriage, only without the horse. Similes — any comparison using the words "like" or "as" — are a lot like analogies, and analogies are self-serving[2]. That is, these kinds of comparisons and little stories are designed to get a specific point across, not to be the end-game of a learning experience. With that in mind, it's okay to gloss over some details as you're diving into a topic.

An automobile is, obviously, quite unlike a horse-drawn carriage. Sure, at the highest possible level they're *similar*, what with the four wheels and the intent to move passengers and cargo, but the analogy tends to break down quickly after that. But when you're trying to quickly relay an important concept at a high level, would you rather be a little inaccurate, or spend twenty minutes explaining the difference between a biological animal and a modern fuel-injected gasoline engine?

I tend to think of learning as an iterative process, meaning you repeatedly come back to the topic in finer and finer detail. Your first pass at a topic is high-level, glossing over a lot of fine details and relying heavily on not-wholly-accurate analogies to get the point across. Some inexperienced, obsessive-compulsive instructors balk at this, feeling that they're essentially lying to their students. I don't see it that way, provided that, within the same learning session (say, a week-long class or whatever), you're looping back and clarifying any egregious misconceptions your initial analogy may have created. You can even say, right up front, "well, I mean, obviously it's not exactly like that, but it's a close enough comparison for now,

---

[2]Even this one.

and we'll dig into the details a bit down the road."

This ties back to our brains' ability to only ingest so much new material in a sitting. If every new idea or concept has to be explained in 100% accurate, excruciating detail, we'd never get anywhere. So gloss over the fine details at first, if you need to, so that you can establish some common ground. Teach *just enough* for now, and return to it later to clarify and dig deeper. "Returning later," not incidentally, plays well into our brains' neural structure, right? By initially establishing a simple, easy-to-recall concept, we create an initially strong synaptic connection between the associated neurons. By returning to that later, we strengthen those connections, and add a few more with some deeper detail. When we return yet again, we strengthen what came before and tack on a bit more. We learn in *layers*, building the onion from the inside out.

Part 4: Constructionism

Constructionism is an instructional design technique that, for me, is incredibly successful in taking learners (including adults) from memorization all the way through to application and beyond. It's a bit of a scary technique for some teachers, and definitely so for some learners, so you have to approach it with a bit of caution. But sometimes the things most worth achieving are the hardest, and so I wanted to dedicate a Part of this book to the topic.

A Non-Boring History of Constructionism

Loosely connected to *experiential learning*, which basically means "learn by doing" if I may be permitted to vastly gloss over the details, constructionism is an approach where learners construct their own mental models to understand the topic at hand. It's a discovery-based kind of learning, albeit a very *guided* kind of discovery. The teacher serves more as a *facilitator*, guiding the students through a series of carefully constructed discovery experiences. In each, students are essentially given or pointed to the resources they'll need to complete a small project, and then let loose on their own or in very small groups. There's rarely a lecture, unless there are some core concepts or goals that need to be delivered first. There are never step-by-step instructions; the whole point is to create an environment that invites failure-and-recovery, which is how our brains ultimately learn best.

Constructionism was first formally defined by Syemour Papert in a proposal to the National Science Foundation, entitled *A New Opportunity for Elementary Science Education*[3]. Papert has gone to pains[4] to point out that constructionism is more complex than just giving students some task and setting them free; while that's certainly a good elevator-pitch way of describing the theory, there's actually a lot of instructional design and thinking that needs to go into it. Papert's work[5] was mainly focused on children, but I've found it to be incredibly useful in teaching adults. My first use

[3]Sabelli, N. (2008). Constructionism: A New Opportunity for Elementary Science Education. DRL Division of Research on Learning in Formal and Informal Settings. pp. 193-206.

[4]Papert, S.; Harel, I (1991). "Constructionism". Ablex Publishing Corporation: 193–206.
[5]Mindstorms: Children, Computers, and Powerful Ideas

of constructionism was out of sheer necessity: I needed to write a computer programming textbook for classes where the teacher would have little subject matter knowledge. Turning the teacher into a *faciliator*, and stressing the need for self-created learning models, was the only way to make it happen.

Core Tenets of Constructionism

The main idea behind constructionism is to give learners some well-scoped project to work on in the topic being taught, and to expose them to whatever adjunct resources they might need to solve the problem. For example, to teach someone to learn to change a tire, you'd put a tire-changing manual in front of them, along with a pile of the necessary tools, and let 'em have at it. Although, that's not *quite* the end of it. In reality, you'd probably just give them a car with a flat tire and ask them to make it drivable again. You see, constructionism is ideally about larger-scale outcomes than it is smaller, intermediate tasks. Nobody *wants* to change a tire; that's not an *outcome*. Changing the tire is the *means* to the outcome, which is being able to drive the car. People *want* to be able to drive their cars, which is what makes that an outcome.

Starting with that big-picture outcome is a key to constructionism, and it's what helps people learn to an *application* level rather than simple memorizing a series of steps. It also allows each learner's unique brain to construct a worldview that is uniquely theirs, rather than trying to win them over to the teacher's worldview. Some learners might figure out how to operate the jack first; others might try to loosen the lug nuts without jacking the car up first. That "choose your own adventure" process lets each brain approach the problem in its own way, which makes each brain more receptive to whatever solutions it comes up with. You're bypassing "the filter," this way, because you're not hanging out information that might be filtered. All the information that's *constructed* (see what I did, there?) is being built *internally*, inside the filters.

Learners also need to know that failure is an option, and that that's okay. This is a big thing to overcome, because people naturally get frustrated when they see others around them succeeding and perceive that they, themselves, are failing. They're looking stupid, they know it, and they don't like it. That's why, as a practical matter, constructionism needs to start off small, with things you know a learner can succeed at, and then built into bigger and bigger things. It means that initial tasks are almost "gimmes," and perhaps not entirely in keeping with constructionism's goals, so that you can create some trust and even a sense of play in the learning environment. This is *especially* important with fear-avoiding adult learners.

You also need to be very careful about matching tasks and the learners' cognitive readiness. In the real world, this usually boils down to being *extremely* clear about learning prerequisites, and being *very* careful to enforce your prerequisites. If a learner isn't ready for what you're trying to teach, then trying to wedge them in anyway is just going to create a frustrating experience for everyone.

Constructionism also insists that learners have time to reflect on what they've learned, and I've found that friendly, open discussions are a good way to do that. "So, did anyone try anything that they definitely wouldn't try again?" "Did anyone do something and then later decide doing it in a different order would have been better?" Turn learners into teachers, and get them to not only explain the problem, but explain how they solved it, and what did and didn't work.

Finally, you ideally want to give students a slightly different context in which to use the same skills they just developed. Perhaps they now need to change a bicycle tire, or a motorcycle tire, or a truck tire, or a wheelbarrow tire. They'll need some of the same stuff that they used on the car, but they'll also need different stuff for each new scenario. This process reinforces the core things they're learning, and helps them construct a larger worldview, which is a key step on moving them toward synthesis and evaluation. Variations on a theme let the brain strengthen core memories through repeated recall and use, while letting it expand the network of neurons that hold each memory, creating a new and bigger story for itself.

Adult-Related Pitfalls of Constructionism

One of the reasons constructionism works is that it leverages two of the most deeply embedded portions of our brains, with regard to learning. First, it gives us a *practical goal* to work toward. It puts us into a situation, and our brains work best in concrete situations, rather than in abstract concepts. Second, constructionism *lets us fail.* We learn the very, very best when we can try something, fail, and then work our way through the failure to the successful outcome of whatever we're doing. Everything we try, and fail at, contributes to a more-complete mental map of whatever topic we're learning. Failure is perhaps the most crucial aspect of constructionism, and it's why you need facilitators rather than teachers: learners need the time and space to fail.

This works fairly well for kids, who have fewer preconceived notions of what learning "should" look like, are less inclined to fear failure, and who are more likely to be in a formal learning environment where the amount of time they spend learning is externally controlled, and not a personal concern. With adults, it's the exact opposite. We already have a notion of what learning "looks like," and constructionism usually ain't it. We're used to the day-to-day pressures that time places on all of our activities, and so constructionism-based learning seems like a waste of time. We get frustrated, asking the facilitator why they "can't just tell me what the answer is?" Finally, and most importantly, the one thing constructionism absolutely relies on — failure — is the one thing adults try to avoid with three times more vigor than they try to succeed.

Making adults successful with constructionism requires, in my experience, a more moderated and guided approach. You can still "do" constructionism, you just have to do it carefully. You almost have to let it sneak up on your adult learners. I call my approach *MicroConstructionism*.

MicroConstructionism

I want to first point out that this isn't the right approach for every situation. While it's laudable to say that you want every learner to achieve application-level learning and beyond, the reality is that you don't always have the time, the right learner audience, or the right tools. Sometimes, various other considerations are going to make you have to compromise and just "train" people to follow a list of steps.

However, when I *can* engage in higher-level teaching, MicroConstructionism is my choice.

Set the Stage

It starts like this: I get very up-front with my learners about what's going to happen.

> This is not an ordinary class, folks. I'm to just going to stand here and talk at you, and then let you follow some step-by-step lists of tasks and call that a "hands-on lab." In fact, I'm going to talk very little. We're going to work through a series of small, mini-projects together, and you're by and large going to be on your own for each one. At the end, I'm going to do a little critique of your work, and we're going to discuss what we all did the same, or differently. Then we'll move on.

> I'm going to make sure you have every tool and reference you could possibly need to be successful. But I won't be holding your hand. You're going to screw up, and you'll probably become stuck at some point. That's

literally the point of this. If you're not failing, you're not learning.

I ask that you do only two things consistently through the class: when you do feel completely stuck, ask me for a hint. That's what I'm here for. I may just direct you to a particular reference or tool and see if you can figure it out, but I'm not going to let you flounder forever. But that failing process is really why we're here. And, I ask that you tell me when you think you're done, so that I can offer some suggestions on your work.

I realize this isn't how classes have gone for you in the past. I promise, though, that if you stick with this and give it a shot, you're going to come out the other end a lot smarter, and a lot more capable. Now, for anyone who's here just because their boss made them come, and not because they're really passionate about this topic, this might not be a great experience for you. I apologize, and I don't mind at all if you follow along to whatever degree you like, and then work on whatever else you might want to work on. You get to decide how much you take away from this experience, and I'll respect and support your decision.

I do ask, though, that you respect the fact that I really do know what I'm doing, here. I'm not interested in teaching you to be a trained monkey who just follows a list of tasks. I can't give you that list for everything you're going to need to do in the real world. But if you play along, you're going to be much better equipped to really do this, on your own, in the real world.

It's a big intro, and I try to keep at as frank and transparent as possible. Folks who just want to go through the motions can occupy themselves however they like.

Start Small

A lot of adults — more than you might realize — immediately get a little fearful, so you might wonder why I put them so on the spot on that intro. That intro is for the folks who weren't there to learn, but who were just there to get some time away from the job. I wanted to let them know up front that I'm not going to cater to them by "training" them when I'd rather be *teaching* them.

To swiftly allay everyone's fears, I immediately launch the class into the first, tiniest project I can possibly come up with. It'll require the least introduction possible, the least tools, and the least reference materials. It should be something almost any of them could do with minimal learning, but not so simple that any of them could complete it immediately with zero work. They need to feel like they've put *some* investment into it, but still get an almost-immediate reward. That first project should lead into the next one, but shouldn't take more than 30 minutes. I monitor the learners closely, because this is my first opportunity to gauge them. If I plan 30 minutes and they all finish in 10, then I've got a good idea how the rest of the class will go. If none of them finish in 30, then I know I've got a level-setting problem, and I may need to adjust how much I'm able to cover in the rest of the class.

Change the tire on this car is the level of project you're looking at for the first one. You might need to read a bit of the car manual to learn how, and you'll need some minimal tools, but you should be able to finish within half an hour. This isn't a true constructionism task, because you're not giving your learners an *outcome* like "make the care drivable," but the goal is to ease into constructionism with a small step that demonstrates to your learners that they can manage this.

Structured Sequences

Many learners, especially adults, will go into a kind of brain-lock if you give them a large, outcome-based project goal right at the outset. "Make a car!" is just too much; even, "make this car drivable" is probably too big a leap at first. Most of us just aren't taught to enjoy taking huge mega-tasks and breaking them down.

And so, to keep the learner motivated and engaged, I'll do the "breaking down" for them, at least in the early stages. As we progress, the projects they're given will be progressively higher-level, and they'll get longer to work on each one. The idea is to build confidence in the methodology, create engagement and enthusiasm for the project, and get their brains thinking outside the "training box."

Some tips:

- I try to have each project be 1.5x to 2x longer than the previous one. So a 30-minute project is followed by a 45-minute to 1-hour one, followed by a 90-minute to 2-hour one, and so on. Sometimes, I'll end up with a couple of one-hours in a row, and that's fine; this is a guideline and goal, not a hard rule.
- I'll start the class by showing the end result of whatever it is we're building together. It's good for people to have the completed vision in their minds.
- Each project must logically follow the one that preceded it. In other words, they should build, gradually. If the overall goal is "make the car drivable," step 1 can be to change the tire. Step 2 might be to evaluate the engine. Step 3 might be to change a spark plug, after the evaluation reveals it's bad. Step 4 might be to re-evaluate and replace a leaking hose.

The idea is to keep them moving, always forward, by building in small steps.

The Anatomy of a Project

So for each of these little projects you set your students on, create a consistent structure for them. This helps give students some reliable frameworks in this scary and unreliable world of constructionism. For example:

1. I will show them the expected outcome. In cases where there might be many legitimate variations, I'll take care to point out that what I'm showing is only one possible outcome. I'll even review what some of the variations might be.
2. I'll introduce them to any new reference materials that they'll be using in the project, and spend some time discussing how the reference is organized and used.
3. I'll introduce any new tools, along with references on how to use those tools.
4. I'll carefully outline what's expected in this project. *Scope* is an important thing to get right, because students need to be able to know when they're done, and when they're not. So the project goal needs to be something that anyone can objectively measure and verify.
5. I'll set them loose.
6. As they work, I try to answer questions not with a direct answer, but by asking them where in the references they might look to find the answer. I'm always encouraging them to self-learn; if they get stuck with the reference material, I'll help with that. Otherwise, I'm more likely to answer their questions with other questions, to try and get them to think about how to solve the problem on their own.
7. When we finish, I always try to review everyone's work, discuss what different people did differently and why, and discuss any variations in the outcome they may have discovered.

When learners are working together in pairs or small groups, I always mix them up after a project. This provides better cross-pollination of ideas, and helps keep one group from becoming a marked under- or over-performer. I'm always very hesitant to use groups or even pairs, because it's too say for one strong personality to "take over" and diminish the fail-to-learn experience for everyone else. Mixing them up helps to mitigate that, and I also am careful to observe group dynamics and identify any strong personalities. Those folks get moved around more frequently so that everyone is forced to fail-to-learn.

Part 5: Nine Learning Killers

There's a lot you can do to create a better learning environment and experience, but there's a lot you can do to make them worse, too. In this Part, we'll explore some of the "don'ts" of instructional design, as well as some of the built-in behaviors that can get in the way of learning.

1. Overteach

Teach students what they need to know, right then. Don't try to teach what you, as the instructor, want them to know.

It's easy to bring your own agenda into a class. After all, you're the instructor — you literally set the agenda. But the biggest area where I see instructors fail is in teaching what they want students to know, not what students need to know.

Most instructors and instructional designers are familiar with the idea of setting and communicating objectives. If your class is broken into modules, or your book is broken into chapters, you typically start out by stating your objectives. One of my publishers, Manning, has a standard where each chapter starts with a bullet list titled "In this Chapter." Microsoft Official Curriculum modules start with a module overview that includes the module objectives. Those objectives are what you plan to teach.

Most instructional designers will also agree that objectives should be active, which is why you'll often see rules like "objectives must start with a gerund." So, an objective like "SQL Server auditing" wouldn't be acceptable, but one like "Configuring SQL Server auditing" would be fine, because it starts with a gerund. That's supposed to make the objective seem more active. I'm not teaching you the feature, I'm teaching you how to configure the feature. That's a task you complete. It's a good objective.

Well, no. It isn't. Nobody wakes up in the morning with a hankering to do that. Configuring, and a huge number of other objectives I see in courses, is a means to an end. It's what you do in order to achieve what you woke up hankering to do. It's a step. A process.

I dislike objectives in courses and in books. Each instructional unit — each chapter, or module, or lesson, or whatever you call it —

should focus on one need. What is it that the student needs to accomplish? Title the instructional unit to clearly describe the need you're meeting, and everything else falls into place.

As an aside, instructional designers do have language for this concept. In their terms, I'm setting the chapter title as a terminal objective, and I might use one or more enabling objectives to get there. I still think that structure leaves a lot of room for an instructor to get sidetracked, though. I'd rather state what it is I'm going to teach you, and then ensure that every single word out of my mouth, or on the page, leads directly to that goal.

I might title a chapter something like, "Capturing User Activity by Using SQL Server Auditing." That's a statement of something a student might truly want and need to know — how to capture user activity. It's a job task. It's a human-level task, something the boss might tell you to do. It scopes the chapter to a particulate technical feature, but the statement is clear about the real-world ability you're going to be learning.

You then have to be really, really careful about what you teach to lead to that goal. The line between what the instructor wants to teach and what the student needs to know can be really fine.

Let's take a non-technical example. I'm teaching a class, and we've gotten to a module I've named "Using a Car to Drive to the Supermarket." That's a pretty clear title, although instructionally I may have several sub-tasks I need to teach: starting the car, putting it into reverse, and so on. Those are things the student needs to know in order to achieve the goal stated in the module's name. You can't get to the market without starting the car and learning to steer it in different directions.

As an instructor, I want my students to be well-informed. I want them to be smart. I also want to impress them with my own knowledge, so that they think I'm smart and give me a good evaluation at the end of class. And so I decide that they need to know how the brakes on the car work. You depress the brake pedal, an electrical signal goes to the master brake cylinder, and that cylinder compresses and pushed brake fluid to the brakes.

Wrong.

Students do not need to know that. Knowing that information does not in any way help them achieve the goal stated in the name of the module. It might help them with other goals, like troubleshooting or fixing the brakes, but that wasn't the deal we made with them when we named the module. What they need to know is that you stomp on the brake pedal and the car stops. That's it.

Here's why: human brains can only absorb a certain amount of information in a given period of time. After that, those brains literally need to sleep on it, allowing the brain's natural background processes to organize the new data, make relations and connections to existing data, and get everything neatly filed in the neural data store we call "memory." Feed someone too much information at once, and the brain goes into an automatic triage mode: I can't possibly remember all of this. Let's see if I can figure out what's important, and I'll just store that. The problem is that this triage mode isn't under conscious control, so the student doesn't get to decide what's extraneous and what's vital. The brain makes that decision almost instantly, based on its ability to connect new information with existing information. In other words, the student's brain might decide that the whole tangent on master brake cylinders was the important bit, and not actually capture the critical fact that stomping on the brake stops the car.

So you must not introduce extraneous information. Teaching isn't about what you want someone to learn, it's about what they need to learn in order to absorb the skills that you promised to deliver when you sold them the class, the book, or whatever.

I teach a lot of Microsoft Official Curriculum courses. Microsoft has a lot of challenges when it comes to courseware, not the least of which is the highly variable quality and approach of their certified trainers. In one instance, I was teaching a class that had previously been taught by another guy at the same facility. That man knew this material cold, and a lot more besides. He knew the product inside-out, upside-down, and sideways. He took every minute of the recommended delivery time, and then some, running students from 8:00am to 5:00pm every day, and even shortening lunches sometimes to pull in extra time.

When I taught the class, we went from 9:00am to 3:00pm, had a full hour for lunch, and my students were measurably better at retaining and applying the skills that the course had promised to teach.

The difference? I threw in no tangents. I added no extra information. I didn't try to prove I was smarter than anybody, and I taught the class with no regards for what I wanted the students to learn. I took the course's top-level outline — what students had seen when they paid for the class — as what they needed to learn, and I taught nothing that didn't directly lead to those needs. The fact that I had a shorter day kept my students fresher, meaning they didn't hit the "fatigue wall" in the afternoon and stop learning outright. Their brains didn't have to go into triage mode and start indiscriminately dropping new information. They walked away feeling more confident that they'd captured everything I'd taught, because I hadn't overloaded them with a firehose of information.

When I first started writing, I wrote long-form IT books. I had no real page count limit, and these things would be 600, 800, or even 1,000 pages long. Then I managed to land a monthly column in a trade magazine, where I'd be allotted just 800 words each month. My editor at the time, Keith Ward, told me that writing an 800-word column would make me a better writer pretty quickly, because I'd learn the precious value of every single word. He was correct. These days I have trouble writing books of more than 300 or 400 pages, because I've learned to be more concise, and to stay on-topic. My books are better not because they're shorter, but because they do a better job of teaching — in large part because they're more concise. That's the real purpose of the principle I'm writing about, here: be concise.

There's another lesson here, which is the implicit contract created between an instructor or author and his students or readers. When you name a chapter, or provide a list of objectives, or whatever, you're promising to deliver just that. If students walk away feeling like they haven't learned that, then they feel cheated — even if the "failure" was you pushing so much information at them that their brains couldn't cope. In other words, if you over-teach, you may well fail to deliver on that implicit contract.

The implicit contract is also important in preparing the brain to learn. These are the things you will know, you're telling each student. This is what I will teach you. That statement can actually help position their brains to learn those things — provided you stick to the contract and don't wander off-message.

This brain behavior is built-in, and you see it used in all kinds of different situations, often to great effect. Magicians, for example, rely heavily on the fact that our brains will look for whatever we're told to look for — and they use that to distract us while they're palming the card or getting a dove from their coat pocket. The minute our brains are told what to expect, we start subconsciously looking for that. So it's important that, once you've created the contract on what a module or chapter will cover, you immediately start delivering on that contract. Every concept you introduce must be explicitly connected to what you said you'd teach.

"I'm going to teach you how to stop a car. Before I get into the actual procedure, I need to talk a bit about momentum, because the concept of momentum is going to affect the procedure." In that sentence, you're acknowledging that you're about to seemingly go off-topic, but you're immediately providing a connection back to the promised topic. "The more momentum you have, the harder you will have to brake in order to stop the car at the same stopping point." Now you've firmly connected the procedure to your tangent. More momentum, more braking, students' brains will think. Got it.

Now you can go into more detail about what momentum is — but keep it relevant. Don't discuss Isaac Newton — he may have discovered momentum, but he does nothing to further the contracted goal of stopping the car. Keep the momentum diversion as brief as possible: "The faster your car is going, the more momentum you build up. That momentum must be reduced to zero in order to stop the car. The brakes can reduce momentum, but the more you've built up, the faster you'll have to reduce it in order to stop at a given point."

So what about student curiosity? What about the student who is really clever, totally grasps what you're teaching, and wants to know some of the underlying details?

Curiosity is good, and should be encouraged — but not at the expense of the less-curious in class. Instead of going off on a more-detail tangent just to prove that you, as the instructor, really do know this stuff, encourage independent exploration. Build "further reading" references into your instructional materials, and encourage curious students to explore. By doing so, you'll achieve two goals. First, curious people usually enjoy independent exploration, and by encouraging it you're encouraging a smarter person. Independent exploration engages a number of higher brain functions, and often helps a student's brain better cement new knowledge. Second, you're keeping the rest of the class on-track. Unless you and the curious student can leave the room — something not possible in a book, by the way — you're putting your tangent in front of everyone. Folks will listen to even a "private" in-class conversation, to be sure they're not missing something, and now you're bombarding everyone with extra information. Brain goes into triage mode, class success level goes down.

In books, tangents are often styled as sidebars. They're often set aside visually in some way, perhaps with a gray background or in a box. Readers are often told to ignore them. The *Dummies* books (and I did write one of those) label them as something like, "Dumb

Stuff You Don't Need to Know." Problem is, you can't stop someone from reading, and they'll often do so because they fear "missing" something. If they don't need to know it, don't put it in the book. Period.

Many of the classes I teach include remote students. Early on, I would shut off my microphone during labs, so that I could discuss issues with each student individually. I relied on the full-room microphone in the ceiling to let remote students know I was still in the room. I'd get into "expanded" discussions with a curious student, and the remotes would invariably, to a person, complain that they couldn't hear me. I wasn't talking to them, but they were worried they were missing something. Once I realize that I was breaking my own rule of not introducing tangents, I stopped doing the side discussions. Maybe on breaks, or during lunch, outside the classroom, where it's more clear that the conversation is private, but never in class.

Mick was right: you can't always get what you want. But if you try sometimes, you might find you get what you — or rather, your students — need. When you begin a new unit of instruction, clearly state what students will learn. Do so in terms that are meaningful to the student's life — state goals that represent real-world tasks and abilities. Ensure that every word out of your mouth, or every word written on the page, ties directly to that goal. Teach nothing that does not apply directly to that goal. Teach what they need, and not what you want them to know.

Students have a limited ability to learn in a fixed period of time. Make sure you're focusing on the most crucial items, and teach only those. You'll help students be more effective when you take on the responsibility of triaging the information.

2. Don't Tell a Story

Remember that our brains are designed to construct stories, based largely on causality, to help us learn. *Cause-effect* is deeply embedded in who we are. A great way to make learning less effective, then, is to forget that.

This is an example I've touched on before, but it's so common I'll bring it up again. It's *incredibly* common to see newer instructional designers try to front-load concepts. *Before I can teach you about car maintenance, I need to go into the whole history of the combustion engine, Henry Ford's assembly line concepts, and so on.* Even if you "tell a story" about those things, you're not helping someone achieve the outcome they came for. You're not placing *them* into the story, because that particular story has no place for the learner. You're not even telling them how all of that prologue material will eventually help them be better at car maintenance.

The dangerous part about this, and the reason it remains a pernicious problem in the world of adult education, is that human brains are *very* good at learning. You can give someone a horribly designed set of learning materials and in many cases they'll still be able to learn. They might not learn as well, and they might not learn as fast, and they might not retain as much, but we rarely measure those things. So it can *seem*, from the outside, like people can learn equally well no matter how badly you design the experience. That's obviously not true, though.

One reason I think storytelling doesn't get as much respect as it should is that it's just harder. Take nearly any topic that an adult might want to learner and it's simply easier to create an outline where you lay out some background concepts, and then lob facts at the learners until their eyes bleed. Break for lunch, repeat. Issue a certificate, class complete. It's *easy*. Building a story is *hard*.

Building a story requires you to triage what you're going to teach, because the nature of storytelling limits how much you can do. Those are *good* limits, because they reflect they very real biological limits of our brains, but *not* storytelling is nice because it lets you ignore those limits and just firehose facts at people.

Consider a brainstorming session, where you and some other experts are creating a course that will teach people how to frame a wall. During a brainstorming session, it's poor form to say "no;" you just let the ideas come and try to capture them all. So you might get a list like this:

- Compressive strength of wood
- Torsion strength of wood
- Building codes regarding stud spacing
- Wall top and bottom plate attachment
- Calculating nail type for a given load
- How to operate a pneumatic nail gun
- How to toe-nail a stud into a floor plate
- Building code requirements for fire breaks
- Maximum wall span for load-bearing walls

And so on. That's great, and you could absolutely build a table of contents from all that. It might look like this:

1. Understanding Loads and Limits

    1. Compressive strength of wood
    2. Torsion strength of wood
    3. Nail pull and shear strength
2. Understanding Building Codes

    1. Stud Spacing
    2. Fire Breaks

3. Wall span lengths
3. Building Techniques

1. Using nail guns
2. Toe-nailing techniques
3. Wall and top plate attachment

For a *reference book,* that might be a great table of contents. References aren't designed to *teach,* they're designed to help you *remember things,* and those things are usually facts and figured. References are a good and necessary thing in many fields. But they don't *teach.*

If my outcome, my end goal, is to learn to frame a wall, where does "compressive strength of wood" come into my story? It probably doesn't. I'm not looking to engineer new building codes. Go out into the world and look at homes being built. The people framing the walls pretty demonstrably are not concerned about torsion and compression. Building codes? Absolutely, they probably have them memorized. But *is that where they started* when they learned to frame a wall? Does memorizing building codes make a sensible start to my story? Probably not. And this is why so many instructional designers eschew storytelling. It's harder.

I'd probably start the story with a brief mention of what walls are designed to do, like supporting a roof and separating rooms. I might show how a single horizontal piece of wood, with enough weight applied to the middle, cracks in half. That's a *problem,* I'd point out, and then I'd introduce vertical studs as the solution to that problem. We'd put a couple of studs into a long span and show how, with enough weight, the top horizontal span still breaks. A *problem.* I'd ask my learners to consider a solution, and they'd doubtlessly arrive at "more studs, spaced closer together." I'd introduce the building codes that mandate studs be 16" on center, and go through an exercise of measuring out 16" intervals on a floor plate. I'd point out that the floor plate was pretty apt to slip and slide all over. A *problem.* So we'd discuss properly attaching it to the base, and that would lead naturally to the discussion on toe-nailing the studs in place. Of course, we'd need to use the nail gun for that, and I'd start by nailing a mannequin hand into a piece of wood. Well, that's a problem — what if that'd been *your* hand? On to proper use of a nail gun, and then back to toe nailing.

All of these things fit into the story. They make sense; they're all needed to achieve the terminal objective of "frame a wall." But I've left stuff out. I don't need to teach about wood loads and such; building codes do that for me, and make it unnecessary for a practitioner to know or care. Only the things that lie I the direct path from my learner's starting point ("I don't know how to frame a wall") to their end point ("I know how to frame a wall") get covered. Anything else is a tangent, and doesn't belong in my story. Everything in my story is *relevant* to my learner, and I've made that clear by introducing them to the problems that each of these things was meant to solve. I've made it *personal.* I've also made it hands-on, which helps develop stronger synaptic connections much faster, so I'll be a lot more confident in my learners' ability to recall these things. And, knowing me, I actually let them *look up* things like stud spacing and nail gun safety from references I provides, so they've constructed their own personal mental model of how to remember these things, along with learning how to use those important references in the future.

That's how you design for people when you want them to really learn.

3. Forget to Level-Set

When instructional designers talk about storytelling, one thing that often comes up is a phase like, "know who your learner is at the beginning of the story, and carefully define who they will be at its end." Most of us are okay at the second part: it's easy to list the real-world tasks that we want someone to learn to accomplish, for example, and those become our learning experiences' *terminal objectives*. That's *terminal* as in, *end*; it's the end goal for the course.

But not everyone is so good at the first part, where we define who our learners are *before* the story begins. What have they already learned to do in life, that would be relevant to our story? What problems are they facing that have brought them to us to learn? If the terminal objective is a task, *why* do they want to perform that task?

These questions tell us a lot about who will be able to learn from what we've got to teach. Let's take framing a wall again: if my learners are 16 year-old kids, I'm going to build a very different story than if they're 30 year-old men and women, right? Those two audiences have very different backgrounds and experiences. I'm going to have to use different analogies to find common ground with those two audiences, and it's likely I wouldn't be as successful if my learning experiences included people from both groups. They might both have the same outcomes in mind, but they're starting in very different places, which means they're going to have different journeys, which means they're going to need different stories.

Learners also deserve to have expectations about where they're going. If an 18 year-old is hoping to get a job in construction, that's very different from a 40 year-old who's looking to do a little do-it-yourself home remodeling. They're going to expect different outcomes from their learning experience, and so I need to start out by understanding that expectation, and being very clear about whether or not the experience I've designed is going to meet that outcome. I also need to be clear about what the story won't cover. "You're going to be learning to frame a wall. Now, I need to point out that this is focused on basic residential framing. Commercial building have whole different sets of rules. We're also not going to be looking at any of the licensing or permitting that might be required, even for a small do-it-yourself project. This is just the basic mechanics of framing. It'll be good for adding an interior partition wall to your house, for example." That helps put everyone on the same page with what they'll truly be able to *do* when they're finished with me.

This doesn't mean you need to fill your introduction with disclaimers; you're not trying to "cover your ass" or anything. But you do need to make sure you're giving an accurate description of what an expected outcome would be, and make sure you're clearly stating where you expect your learners to be starting. "I'm assuming you're already skilled with basic hand tools like hammers, and that you know how to use basic personal protective equipment like gloves and safety glasses. I'm also assuming you're mainly into this for home DIY projects, not for something larger or something commercial."

Just get everyone on the same page *up front*, both with where you're starting, and where you're going.

4. Wreck the Delivery

I wrote in the front of this book that I regard instructional design, authoring, and delivery to be distinct things, and that I wasn't going to touch on delivery much. *Much.*

The reality is that instructional delivery is where the rubber meets the figurative road, and the best way to kill a well-designed course is to let a poor instructor deliver it. So it's worth thinking, *as a designer*, about how to build learning experiences that easily lend themselves to a good delivery, while requiring an effort to botch the delivery. It's not absolute and it's not foolproof, but it can make all the difference in "borderline" situations. A bad delivery isn't necessarily the designer's fault, but a good designer can do a lot to mitigate a bad delivery.

First, sequencing your material into a well thought-out storyline is the best defense against a bad delivery. With a tight enough storyline, you make it difficult to teach things out-of-order without it not being really apparently awkward. Provide delivery notes that *really* discourage instructors from going off on tangents. Plenty will want to do so, in part because it makes them feel like they're "adding value" to the course rather than just reciting it, and because it lets them demonstrate their expertise. You can't stop that desire, but you can manage it. Try to anticipate the tangents you can, and provide an explicit place for them. Perhaps that's at the end of the learning experience, or perhaps it's in "sidebars" that you position at the end of a learning session. Yes, I've already discussed how I generally dislike sidebars, but we're talking about compromise, here. By positioning "sidebars" at the end of a session, you can at least exercise some control over it. You can call them out as what they are, indicate that it's "above and beyond" information, and help students understand that it's okay to mentally check out of they need to. Encourage instructors to use those sidebar times as the place to show off and add value, and to work with their higher-performing learners to expand their horizons.

Well-designed *instructional aids* can also be useful. For example, providing leading questions that can help an instructor engage their class can keep the environment more engaging and interactive. Providing practical experiences, such as hands-on activities, can be useful, and even more so when they're built in a constructionism style that relies on the instructor to be a facilitator.

Remember, too, that the point of constructionism is largely to take instructors out of the picture and make learners into self-instructors. You'll need to *sell* your instructors on that concept, in most cases, by making a clear case for constructionism and outlining concrete activities and tasks for the instructors to take on. Provide "to-do" lists for instructors, such as having them introduce reference materials or tools at specific points, encourage the use of those at other points, and so on. Continually exhort instructors to give learners the space and time they need to fail and recover on their own. Provide pre-made tips that instructors can relay to learners, for those "I'm stuck" situations that you can anticipate. Providing slide decks, while technically outside the realm of an instructional designer as I've define it, is another way to exercise more control of the delivery experience, minimize unnecessary distractions, and so on.

Another trick — again, because few instructors want to be seen as merely "reading from the book" like a vocalizing monkey — is to provide separate instructor materials that include additional analogies, examples, and sub-stories that students themselves don't receive directly. This allows instructors to "add value" in a way that stays entirely within your overall story arc and instructional framework.

While an instructional designer, again within my limited definition of the role, might not be the one delivering what they design, they *can* help ensure a better delivery by *also designing the delivery itself.* Understanding how instructors approach learning experiences, accommodating *their* needs (just as you do the learners'), and providing a story *for them* is a great way to make a learning experience that ultimately delivers a better win for the people it's meant to benefit the most.

5. Leave Objectives Unstated

I got into this a bit in number 3, above, but I want to go into this idea of terminal objectives a bit more specifically, and with a broader reason in mind.

You should never set out to teach unless you have a *terminal objective* in mind. That is, what is it that you're teaching, and why would a student care? Terminal objectives should be *tasks* in most cases, and should usually be some activity or behavior that an outsider could objectively observe and measure. For example, if you're teaching someone to draw a picture, then that drawing becomes the outcome; if you're teaching someone to create a new traffic plan for an intersection, then the plan is the outcome. Anyone could see that those outcomes exist or not, and so those make final terminal objectives.

Objectives create an agreement, or a contract of sorts, with your learner. They're a promise for why everyone is sitting down and doing all of this. Leaving objectives unstated or implied makes your teacher-learner agreement vague and unknowable. That's bad for learners, because their brains won't know what the point of it all is, and their brains may start accidentally filtering out the wrong information as you go. By knowing the destination up front, learners' brains can focus on that destination, and make sure they're picking up all the intermediate steps along the way.

Terminal objectives also help keep you, as the teacher, honest. For every single thing you add to a learning experience, ask yourself, "how is this moving us directly toward the terminal objectives?" If you answer yourself with something like, "well, it doesn't exactly, but it's still good to know," then you need to drop whatever it is.

Anything that doesn't directly contribute to the terminal objectives doesn't belong: they're tangents, distractions, and an opportunity to exhaust your learners' attention spans. If you've got "nice to know" material you want to share, save it until *after* the terminal objectives are met, in something like an appendix or afterword: "Hey, now that we're done, you might want to also look into this and that and this other thing. They're all great ways to start expanding your knowledge of this topic."

I get into arguments (well, let's be polite and call them "debates") with people about whether terminal objectives should be explicitly called out at the start of a learning experience. Broadly speaking, yes, they should. I never really disagree with anyone on that. Where I disagree is *how* to do so. Say you're writing a module for a course that will be delivered by an instructor, or creating a self-paced learning video, or writing a chapter for a book. *I* believe that those units - the chapter, the video, or the module - should each focus on just one terminal objective. They should be short, usually under an hour apiece, and even shorter if you can pull it off. The *title* of that unit, I believe, is where you communicate the terminal objective: "Planning Traffic Signal Timing," "Changing a Car Tire," "Installing a Vertical Stabilizer," "Changing a Faucet." Those titles start with a *gerund*, an active verb ending in *-ing*. Those are all *tasks*, and they speak to externally observable outcomes. If you do nothing but say the title aloud, any learner should be able to clearly explain what they believe they're about to learn, and what they'll be able to do afterwards. What I don't personally think you need to do is then have a formal slide, page, bullet list, or whatever that spells out the point of the learning session. No, "here's what you'll learn" section, none of that.

I'll often see people list the *enabling objectives* they plan to use. I won't go so far as to say it's wrong, but I do feel it's useless. You've already told the learner, in the title, that you plan to teach them to change a faucet. It should go without saying that they're going to learn to use a basin wrench, for example, or that they're going to use Teflon tape. I don't feel you need to waste time listing all those steps - students will be countering them in a good sequence anyway. Listing those enabling objectives up front is simply dumping information into the learners' brains - information which, at that exact point in time, does them no good at all. Enabling objectives aren't the goal; they're the steps along the way to the goal. Consider the navigation app you've probably used on your phone: *you* state the goal, which is your destination. When you hit "Start," does your phone read off all the turns you're about to make? Nope. It waits until you need each piece of information and reveals it then. Sure, you *could* review the route ahead of time, but unless you're just checking to make sure it's keeping you off the 405 during rush hour (or whatever), there's no real benefit in doing so. That's not an exact analogy, of course, but hopefully you get the idea I'm trying to express.

6. Ignore the Attention Span

You, as a teacher, can't always get what you want, and that's especially true if what you want is for your students to pay close attention for a long period of time. As an instructional designer, one key thing you are responsible for is limiting the scope of what your material attempts in a single learning session, whether that's an hour in a class, a video someone is watching, or a chapter someone is reading. You can't necessarily ensure that the *delivery* will respect the limits you've built into your material, but you can certainly try and do the right thing up front.

Most adults need to know within 5 minutes what they're going to get from a session - that is, they need to know the intended outcome, or terminal objective, that they're aiming for. Once they know it, you've usually got less than 30 minutes to get to the point, and even that's often pushing it. Your total delivery time might be targeted at about an hour, but anything more than *that* probably means your terminal objective is too broad; you need to break it down and teach one thing at a time. For example, "maintaining a car" is too broad; you need terminal objectives that are a bit tighter, like "changing the oil in a car," "checking the tire pressure," and so on. That lets your learners go from zero to a meaningful outcome in under an hour apiece.

That "30 minutes to get to the point" is really important, and you should try and get the actual time as small as possible. What this time cover is usually "background material." For example, teaching "how to change the oil in a car" might require a quick word on why oil is important to the car's engine, so that you can establish the problem that learners will try and solve. You might need to spend a bit of time explaining how oil breaks down over time, and how it picks up dirt and grime, making it less effective at lubricating. You might even show some old and new oil to drive that point home. All that "up front" might take all of 5 minutes, which is perfect - that's well under 30 minutes, and lets you get to the point of actually changing the oil quickly.

So my guidelines are usually:

- Cover background in as little time as possible, definitely under 30 minutes.
- Get to a meaningful outcome in under an hour after you start, including background material coverage time.
- If you can't do this, you need smaller terminal objectives and/or less background material.

7. Lose Touch

(Need to repeatedly assess if your learners are following along, either through formal assessment tools or informal class management, but neither can just be stupid trivia questions. Commit to it.)

8. Train

(Versus teaching)

9. Prevent Failure

(Anticipating failure is great, because you can teach to it; don't try to structure learning in a way that avoid it, because that's how we learn).

Part 6: How I Design: a Case Study

I thought it might be useful to include a chapter, which I'll try to make as concise as possible, on how I actually apply my instructional design approach. Although my own background is in information technology, I'll use a more generic example here, in hopes that'll be more broadly applicable. That said, I don't like to use artificial, dumbed-down examples because you tend to miss a lot of real-world nuance with those.

With all that in mind, let's say I needed to teach someone how to build a framed, insulated, non-load-bearing interior wall. We've all seen a wall before, and we probably all have an idea of what goes into one (studs, nails, insulation, and drywall, mainly). Wall construction is governed by building codes, so there are some background rules and concepts that we need to consider, which I think makes this a pretty decent example.

Outcomes: Terminal Objectives

My first pass at terminal objectives is usually pretty easy:

Build an interior, non-load bearing, insulated wall.

The objective has some obvious built-in limits on scope: we're not building an exterior wall, we are adding insulation, and we're not building a load-bearing wall. Right there, the learner is learning something: there are many different types of wall, and I'm only going to learn to build one kind. I'd probably go a step further and add just a minor detail:

Build a code-compliant, interior, non-load bearing, insulated wall.

This emphasizes my desire to teach someone *the right way* to perform the task, and teaches the learner that there are also *wrong ways*, which I might not be covering. Importantly, this restated objective is *observable*, meaning an informed third party could look at the learner's behaviors and work product and objectively determine if they were able to perform the terminal objective. The objective is based on a real-world verb, *build*; you can see someone build something, and you can test what they've built to see if it was done correctly.

This "feels" like an objective that I can teach in a reasonable period of time. "Build a house" would be too much, right? That would include so many different systems — plumbing, electrical, roofing, flooring, and more — that we'd spend months at it. "Build a wall," however, has the feel of something that we could probably get through in about an hour, which is kind of my starting point for scoping a topic.

Unwinding Dependencies and Prerequisites

Now that hard part begins. I use a kind of "freeform" approach to understanding what I need to teach. Because I'm working with a physical outcome — a wall — I might actually *look* at one to start figuring out what I need to teach.

First, I am *not* going to teach the building code *per se*. My objective isn't, "understanding the building code," it's "build a wall." I'm going to teach someone to build a wall *in a way that complies with code*, and along the way I will probably mention specific bits that have to be done "in order to be compliant with code," but I'm not going to sit down at the beginning of my learning experience and go over the code itself. Building codes are background concepts, in a way, and I don't like to make learners simply memorize concepts up-front. Instead, I'll weave the building codes into the narrative, remaining focused on *what* we're trying to accomplish.

As I start thinking about the things I need to teach, I'll usually use sticky notes, stuck to a wall or whiteboard. This is helpful because I like to reorder them as I think about the order in which I'll teach them. I'll organize them into columns for major subjects, and then each column will represent the order in which I need to teach things. If you've got a big enough table, you could use index cards, and I'm sure the are electronic equivalents (for the record, I don't like using Kanban tools like Trello for this exercise, although I think that's simply because I *like* moving physical slips of paper around when I'm doing this).

For the photos in this book, I used the macOS "Stickies" application, just to give you an idea of how this might look while keeping the screen shot easier to make out.

As I stare at a wall, I start thinking of tasks like:

- Measuring and cutting wood
- Laying out the studs
- Affixing the sill (bottom) plate to the structure
- Affixing the top plate
- Toe-nailing the upright studs to the plates
- Nailing horizontal breaks between studs
- Inserting the insulation badding
- Screwing drywall into the studs

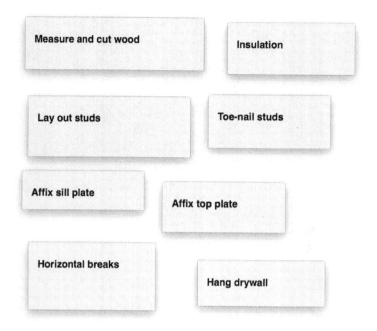

Starting my sticky notes

These just get written on notes or cards, in no particular order. As I think about some of those, from my perspective as an expert wall builder, I realize I'm missing some bits. Before you can hang drywall, for example, you need to attach cardboard shims to the studs, to help even out irregularities and provide a flat surface for the drywall to attach to. So I'll add a card for that.

I also want to add some notes to indicate where I should discuss code specifics. For example, code has rules for stud spacing, toe-nailing guidelines, horizontal break placement, and so on. I'll actually make notes on those cards, so that I remember to bring the code requirements in at the right time.

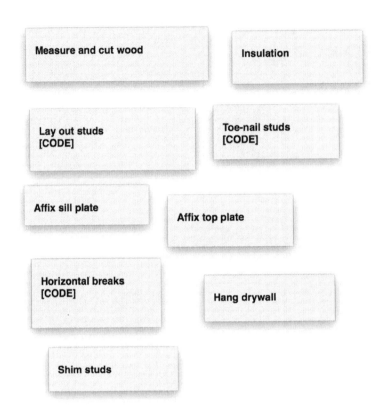

Expanding my notes

Notice that all of my notes, at this point, are *tasks*. I consider these to be *enabling objectives*. By themselves, none of them are real useful in terms of outcomes — being able to lay out studs is, by itself, not something you'd get hired for. But each of them is still an observable, objective activity. Yes, along the way some of those activities include helping the learner *understand* something, such as helping the learner understand that studs have to be spaced 16" on center, and what that means. But learning that background information *is part of learning the task;* I'm not teaching about stud spacing, I'm teaching someone how to properly lay out a wall.

I'm not worried about what *order* any of this is going to go in, yet; I'm just trying to make sure I'm capturing everything. One way to do that is to look at each task and think, "what would someone need to know in order to do this?" If there is something, then I need to decide if I'll teach that, or if I'll make it a prerequisite that learners are expect to know coming in.

For example, consider "measure and cut wood." You're going to need to know how to use a saw, probably a mitre saw. I think that's probably out of scope for my current teaching plan, because using a mitre saw is applicable across a wide range of tasks besides wall-building. Therefore, I'll document that as a prerequisite. Insulation will likely need to be cut; that just involves scissors, which should be basic human knowledge, so I won't bother documenting that or teaching it. Toe-nailing kind of assumes you know how to use a claw hammer at least, and in reality probably assumes you know how to use a pneumatic framing nailer. Hmm. Framing nailers and wall-building are pretty tightly coupled, so I'll include some quick nailer instruction by adding a new card. There are some safety practices I need to include, so I'll note that on the card.

Adding dependencies and prerequisites

I'll continue running through the list, making sure each card's dependencies are either covered by another card, or documented as a prerequisite that I can later communicate to learners before they dive in with me.

Storyboarding, Chunking, and Finding the Arc

Now that I've got a solid idea of *what* I need to teach, I need to start figuring out the sequence. Sequencing is only the first step, but it's an important one. I don't ever want to tell a learner "I'll get to that later;" I don't even want to *mention* stuff until I'm ready to go into it fully.

I'll try to sequence things in the order a practitioner would actually experience them. Cut the wood, get the sill plate down, lay out the studs, nail the studs, and so on. I'll stick notes to each other where I want to start grouping them, like covering nailers and toe-nailing as part of laying out the studs.

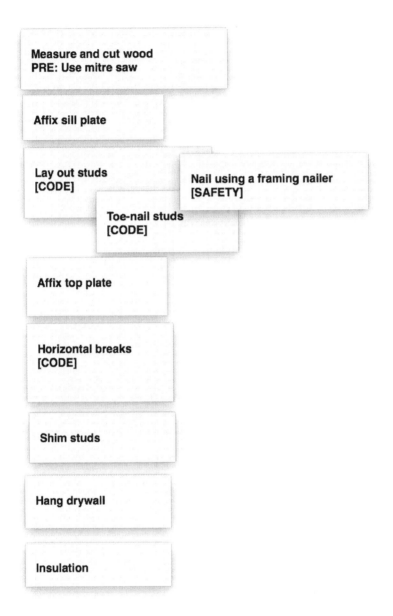

Measure and cut wood
PRE: Use mitre saw

Affix sill plate

Lay out studs
[CODE]

Nail using a framing nailer
[SAFETY]

Toe-nail studs
[CODE]

Affix top plate

Horizontal breaks
[CODE]

Shim studs

Hang drywall

Insulation

Beginning the sequence

This list serves as a kind of storyboard, like you might create when scripting a movie. Each note represents a "scene" in the movie, where we'll experience a specific thing. Each thing leads pretty naturally to the next thing. As you can see, I've got a couple of logical chunks, including a possible chunk where we'll shim and hang the drywall.

Now it's time to find the storyline, or *story arc*. You see, I can't just toss a learner into this — I need to give them something personal to connect to. Are they framing in an entirely new building, or are they just dividing up a large space in their basement into a couple of rooms? The former scenario might require me to go back and cover additional material for that bigger situation; the latter might require me to add more in the way of tool safety and practices, since I could expect the do-it-yourself homeowner to have less experience in that area.

The story arc also provides some specific color for each sticky note. For example, if we're indeed standing up a partition wall in the basement, I might need to discuss how to attach the sill plate to a concrete slab, although for completeness' sake I might also discuss (if not demonstrate) the differences in attaching the sill plate to a wooden subfloor. Thinking about the story helps provide some fine detail, which I'll also note on my cards.

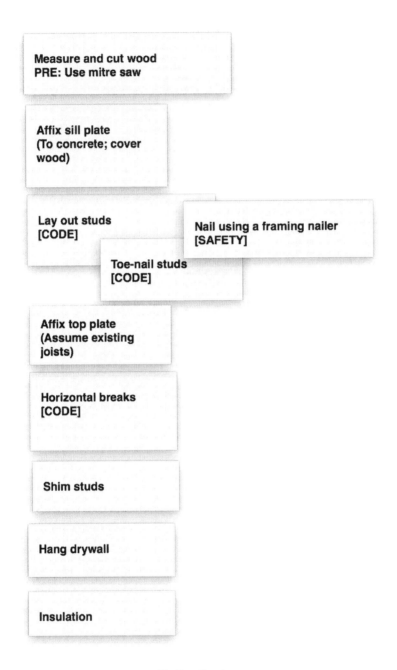

Measure and cut wood
PRE: Use mitre saw

Affix sill plate
(To concrete; cover
wood)

Lay out studs
[CODE]

Nail using a framing nailer
[SAFETY]

Toe-nail studs
[CODE]

Affix top plate
(Assume existing
joists)

Horizontal breaks
[CODE]

Shim studs

Hang drywall

Insulation

Finding the story

Knowing the story, and the intended audience, also helps me develop out the analogies I'll use to explain concepts.

Identifying Concepts and Analogies

I've already identified, on my sticky notes, some of the core concepts I'll need to teach, like the applicable building codes. But there are probably more, and I need to specifically note them (I use [square brackets] to do that). For example, sill plates provide an important function in a wall: they keep the wall from moving, and they form a connection to the existing structure. That's something I need to explain, so that as learners are attaching sill plates, they'll do so in a way that supports those functions.

Stud spacing is more than just a code requirement; the code exists for a *reason*. Stud spacing is calculated to provide the proper level of stiffness in the wall, and to support common overhead loads. Insulating badding is based on stud spacing, so getting the spacing right will make insulation installation easier later on.

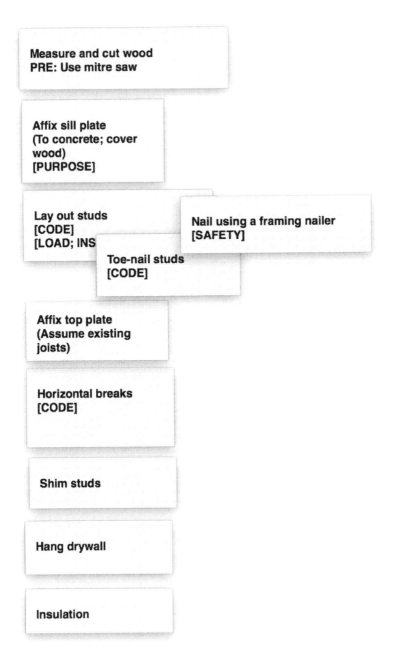

Measure and cut wood
PRE: Use mitre saw

Affix sill plate
(To concrete; cover
wood)
[PURPOSE]

Lay out studs
[CODE]
[LOAD; INS

Nail using a framing nailer
[SAFETY]

Toe-nail studs
[CODE]

Affix top plate
(Assume existing
joists)

Horizontal breaks
[CODE]

Shim studs

Hang drywall

Insulation

Identifying concepts to teach

Identifying all of these concepts, and adding them to the cards, helps me make sure I'm getting all the "background information" I need, and that I'm "attaching" it to the tasks it best belongs with. This is also where I need to start thinking about my analogies, which I'll use to explain these concepts. This is where I'll often start writing, switching from "instructional design" mode to "teacher" mode; even if I'm not drafting out complete analogies, I'm at least making some inroads on how I want to explain each concept to my particular learner audience.

Trial Run

Of course, I almost never get it right the first time. I'll miss dependencies, realize I've got the sequence not-quite-right, and so on. So a trial run is important. I'll often try to start with a small learner audience, and I'll often use draft or incomplete teaching materials. That kind of means "winging it," which I can do because I'm comfortable as a teacher *as well as* an instructional designer; in cases where you're just designing and not teaching, you'll need to collaborate with your "test teacher" to get the minimally viable learning materials in place to do a test run.

Remember, a test run isn't a test of your teaching materials, it's a test of your *structure*. Learner questions will help you uncover things you may have missed, or sequences that need to be rearranged. I don't necessarily mean you need to *anticipate* questions and proactively answer them in your teaching materials, but if your story isn't eventually answering common learner questions, then you need to find an appropriate place in the story for those answers.

I keep my sticky notes until I'm done with my test run, because rearranging is an opportunity to really screw things up if you're not careful. Having the original notes in place lets me look at the complete story arc in one "view," so to speak, so I'm less likely to mess something up by simply tweaking one thing. Instead, I continue to view the whole course as a whole structure.

Instructional design should be a living thing; there's always room to tweak and adjust your story after you've told it a few times. You might decide to tighten up a certain area that's not adding as much value as you'd originally thought; you might decide to expand a certain area that was too terse and was confusing learners.

Afterword

I truly hope this book has offered you some useful perspectives. I personally *love* thinking and learning about how people learn, and how I can do a better job presenting information and new skills to them. Hopefully, this book has helped you start down a road toward doing the same.

Suggested Reading

All of these are a bit more scientific and in-depth than what I've attempted here, and some of these serve as my own resources when I'm working on instructional design.

How We Learn: The Surprising Truth About When, Where, and Why It Happens - Benedict Carey

Instructional Design that Soars: Shaping What You Know Into Classes That Inspire - Guila Muir

ISD From The Ground Up: A No-Nonsense Approach to Instructional Design - Chuck Hodell

Make It Stick: The Science of Successful Learning - Peter C. Brown, et. al.

Made in the USA
Lexington, KY
03 October 2018